Spring Mountain

Spring Mountain:
The Complete Poems of Nansŏrhŏn

Translated by
Ian Haight and T'aeyong Hŏ

WHITE PINE PRESS | BUFFALO, NEW YORK

White Pine Press
P.O. Box 236
Buffalo, NY 14201
www.whitepine.org

Publication of this book was supported by public funds from the New York State Council on the Arts, with the support of Governor Kathy Hochul and the New York State Legislature, a State Agency and the Daesan Foundation.

Acknowledgements: See page 149.

Cover Image: Shin Yun-bok (1758–1814). "Scenery on Dano Day."

Printed and bound in the United States of America.

ISBN 978-1-945680-80-9

Library of Congress Control Number: 2024939689

Spring Mountain

Contents

Introduction

Hŏ Ch'ohŏi (1563-1589), or as she is more commonly known by her penname, Nansŏrhŏn ("white orchid"), is regarded by Korean scholars as among the greatest female poets of Korea. Born into the noble class of 16th century Neo-Confucian Korea, Nansŏrhŏn is respected for her feminism, sympathy to "lower classes," and a superb poetic craft. An account of the circumstances of Nansŏrhŏn's life and the times she was born into is helpful to an appreciation of her poetry.

Confucian Society

According to Korean Neo-Confucianism in the time of Nansŏrhŏn, when a woman married, her husband's family became her true family. All familial ties a woman held before marriage might still be important and influential, but the priority and significance frequently lessened. All previous familial ties were completely severed in rare cases.

A noblewoman as wife and mother was in practiced principle honored and respected by the family she married into. Her status demanded she follow prescribed duties. She served her husband and his mother's everyday needs and sublimated her individuality to the family she married into. Aside from conceiving and bearing children, a noblewoman was expected to achieve honor and respect through negation of her physical and emotional personhood; she was not to display desire, jealousy, or anger. The selflessness of a Korean noblewoman's duties in the 16th century made a conception of self-identity near impossible; the honor and respect conferred allowed no space for a separate being. The higher the honor and the greater the respect, the more conceptual, abstract, and remote became the identity of a noblewoman's person.

These social norms included the fact that a Korean Confucian mother-in-law held near complete authority over the wife of her son. The daughter-in-law had to serve her new mother food and comb her hair. If the newlywed couple spent too much time together, the man's mother might become jealous and quarrel with the daughter-in-law. This was especially true of mothers who had been widowed, neglected by their husbands, or who had in some way a son that was unusual. It is easier to abuse a person who is allowed little or no individuation, and so the well-known mistreatment of the daughter-in-law in Korean folklore is unsurprising.

It is also true an elderly matriarch would, as custom, give all her valued possessions, duties, and responsibilities to the next woman in line for the family matriarchy. The next woman in line was frequently the wife of the family's first-born son. If there was no matriarch of the family, the new wife would assume that position. As matriarch, the new wife's position in the family would be much more favorable in terms of family relationships than if her mother-in-law or grandmother-in-law were still living.

Confucianism in 16th century Korea held that males and females after the age of seven should not sit together. The layout of a nobleman's house was designed to conform to this Confucian view of a family's order, and separated the daily life of the sexes. Noblewomen resided away from the gaze of any male; husbands and wives almost never ate together, although the wife could be present at the husband's meals. Usually, the only men allowed access to a noblewoman's quarters were sons, the husband, or a close relative, while the noblewoman would not normally go to her husband's quarters.

Women's quarters normally had a garden court with flowers, sometimes with a pond which could be enjoyed. According to the house design, a noblewoman would not be able to be seen by people outside the walls of her house. The wealthier a nobleman's family, the more removed his noblewoman wife was from the outside world. On the rare occasion a woman from the upper classes traveled outside her house walls, she did so in an enclosed sedan or wore a full-body veil.

In addition to the hardship of sequestering, Korean noblewomen of the Chosŏn Dynasty were allowed no public formal education, and generally were allowed no private advanced education. This is because to have an education was considered to resemble a "kinyŏ," or courtesan. Upper-class women were discouraged from exploring poetry, painting or calligraphy partly because the kinyŏ or, more commonly, "kisaengs," learned these arts for the sake of performance for men.

Women in upper-class families learned to read and write either through the teachings of a grandfather, father, or brother, in contrast with courtesans who attended courtesan schools. Sometimes a girl from a noble family would be taught at the same time as a brother who was home-tutored. The education girls received under these circumstances could be about their traditional roles as women according to Confucianism, but what was emphasized in the education could vary according to the family.

For the noblewomen who wrote poetry, most of their poems did not survive history. A noblewoman's poetry was shared with close friends or family, and until Nansŏrhŏn, never published. Poems were seldom handed down to posterity; the poetess or parents usually burned her writings so the family reputation would not be damaged. A woman's love poems, for example, could lead to rumors of a wife's unfaithfulness, and she might then be viewed as vulgar or base. There are very rare cases of scholarly noblewomen from the Chosŏn period whose paintings, essays and poetry were revered while the woman lived, but almost always, a woman's work, in the rare case of public presentations, was presented to the world outside the noblewoman's quarters posthumously.

It should not be forgotten that men who were financially able were expected to have concubines or lovers. A married woman or concubine, however, was expected to be loyal to her husband sexually and emotionally, even after his death. A married woman who expressed jealousy over her husband's concubines or lovers could be divorced or abandoned.

Contrasts Between Kisaengs and Noblewomen

The freedoms and limitations accorded kisaengs help illustrate the remoteness of life upper-class Korean women of the Chosŏn Dynasty lived. Although a kisaeng came from lower classes and was an entertainer of men, kisaengs could establish individuality by defining, to a certain degree, how they existed in the culture. A kisaeng developed personality by the way she expressed her style as an entertainer and courtesan. Kisaengs, then, had an avenue to grow as human beings their upper-class female counterparts lacked.

Despite any skill in poetry, music, or painting, kisaengs were not regarded as artists, and were generally perceived as lower class even though a kisaeng might be wealthy. Regardless of the accomplishment of a kisaeng's poems, she would not have any acknowledgment except for that received from the men she entertained. A kisaeng might then have more work or greater material comfort.

Kisaengs were the only class of women allowed to openly associate with men in public. Kisaengs could address men directly and share intellectual and emotional companionship "virtuous" wives could not. Besides poetry and "intelligent" conversation with their male patrons, kisaengs were allowed embellished clothing and accessories. A kisaeng might pretend to like or love anyone, but she was free from having to appear to love one man whom she had no part in choosing, however absent and interested in other women he might be. She might also pretend, as a good Confucian woman should, that she experienced no passion, but she was uniquely free, if she chose, to sing or write of all the passion she felt.

Biographical Information

Nansŏrhŏn was born in the second century of the Chosŏn Dynasty. Her father Hŏ Yŏp (1517-1580) was a scholar and high official. Her mother, known only by her family name of "Kim," was the first and legal wife of Yŏp. Yŏp married Kim after his previous wife, Han, had died. Nansŏrhŏn had two maternal brothers, Hŏ Pong (penname Hakok, meaning "lotus valley" (1551-1588)) and Hŏ Kyun (penname Kyosan, meaning "dragon mountain" (1569-1618)), both of whom are respected writers in the Korean literary tradition.

Nansŏrhŏn was born in Kangnŭng, a village in a pine forest beside a lake; Kangnŭng is on the east coast of Korea's peninsula. She was raised in a fairly open landscape surrounded by water and mostly flatlands of rice fields. Perhaps because of the village's removed locale, Nansŏrhŏn was permitted to be outdoors and play with lower-class children.

Nansŏrhŏn's family was politically and intellectually important. Her father and brothers served as high-ranking ministers and governors, as well as diplomats to Japan and China during periods of war. They also were responsible for some of the most significant literature and literary criticism of the Chosŏn Dynasty, writing that remains relevant to contemporary Korean studies in the humanities.

When Nansŏrhŏn lived, the marriages of Korean noblewomen were arranged for social or political purposes, and typically they married in adolescence. Somewhat atypically, Nansŏrhŏn's husband, Kim Sŏngrip (1562-1592), was chosen not for political alliances but for superstitious reasons. A soothsayer had predicted Nansŏrhŏn would die an early death due to a poor constitution unless she married a "simple" man. Hakok had a close friend by the name of Kim Ch'ŏm, whose son, Sŏngrip, seemed a likely match. Sŏngrip was not a man of remarkable intelligence, although he apparently was kind. The two married in 1577 when Nansŏrhŏn was fourteen.

As was custom, Nansŏrhŏn's in-laws became in practice her most important family, and on infrequent occasions she visited members of her natural family. Her husband's home region was different from Kangnŭng. Her new family house was nestled between two small hills connected to larger interlacing valleys of hills and mountains south of Seoul, perhaps contributing to the theme of confinement in her poems.

The situation of Nansŏrhŏn's marriage was stifling and had a powerful influence on the kind of poems she wrote. Scholars of Korean literature believe Sŏngrip likely was intimidated by Nansŏrhŏn's intellectual acumen. Korean noblemen had mistresses and frequented courtesans, but Kim's neglect of Nansŏrhŏn was acute. After marriage, Kim was seldom home, sometimes leaving Nansŏrhŏn with a hateful mother-in-law for over a year.

There is evidence Sŏngrip had genuine affection for Nansŏrhŏn. He was gone for so long, however, at the request of his mother, who insisted he study for government service exams in Seoul. It is easy to speculate Nansŏrhŏn's mother-in-law was jealous of Nansŏrhŏn's intelligence and resented her husband Ch'ŏm's favoritism towards Nansŏrhŏn. Scholars have suggested Sŏngrip's mother conspired to keep Nansŏrhŏn and Sŏngrip separate. She also blamed Nansŏrhŏn for a litany of family troubles (by bringing "bad luck" to the family), including the death of Ch'ŏm, which occurred during a visit to Nansŏrhŏn's brother Hakok, who was in exile.

Deeper tragedies began to strike Nansŏrhŏn in her late teens and early twenties. In 1580, her father died of an unknown illness while on a journey to Seoul. Hakok, her elder and perhaps most beloved brother, was sent into exile three times in 1583. Nansŏrhŏn lost her son and daughter in 1586 and 1587; she suffered a miscarriage in 1587. In 1588 Hakok returned from exile but was still not allowed into the capital. That same year he died of jaundice after heavy bouts of drinking around Kŭm Kang Mountain; he was still out of favor with the king. The traumas Nansŏrhŏn lived undoubtedly contributed to the emotional tenor of her poetry.

Nansŏrhŏn predicted the day she would die. When the day came, she changed into plain ceremonial clothes and burned all her poems and paintings. Her body was found sitting at her writing table. Nansŏrhŏn died at the age of twenty-seven on March 19th, 1589, and there has been speculation she committed suicide. There is no factual record as to the cause of death.

Nansŏrhŏn, Poet

Nansŏrhŏn's father, Hŏ Yŏp, practiced traditional Confucian principles which maintained women should not receive an education in creative literature like poetry. Nonetheless, he was aware Hakok sponsored this type of education for Nansŏrhŏn, and Yŏp did not prevent it. Hakok, himself an accomplished poet, was interested in the Chinese literature that aligned itself closely with Taoism: the poetry of T'ang Dynasty China. For Hakok, the style of these poets was prized over the prevailing Confucian style of poems in Korea. Nansŏrhŏn's brothers and their group of writers are credited for introducing a new style and aesthetic to Korean poetry of the 16th and 17th centuries. Themes and forms changed, imitating but revising the standards of the Tang poets.

One of Nansŏrhŏn's influential tutors was I Tal (1539-1612). Tal was a lower-class but highly intelligent scholar who could never attain any meaningful position because his mother had been a concubine. Some scholars have claimed Tal's influence is part of the reason for Nansŏrhŏn's interest in those who are oppressed. Tal advocated a writing style and purpose similar to Chinese T'ang Dynasty poets. It was a literary act of rebellion against the Chinese Song Dynasty style then prevalent in Korea and practiced by the titled-by-bloodline nobility. This meant Nansŏrhŏn was instructed in the poetry of Li Bai, Du Fu, and Wang Wei, among many other T'ang poets. Nansŏrhŏn probably also became familiar with the Chinese "Women Poets of Anguish," a tradition of poetry written by Chinese noblewomen or courtesans who found themselves in circumstances like those Nansŏrhŏn encountered after marriage.

Nansŏrhŏn was certainly a genius and likely a child prodigy. She is believed to have written her first long and complex hansi—which is the Korean use of classical Chinese to write poetry—in 1570 at the age of eight (the first poem in this manuscript, "Upon the Raising of the Frame for White Jade Pavilion in Great Galaxy Palace"). Himself an accomplished poet, Hakok actively encouraged Nansŏrhŏn to write and paint, even after her marriage. Perhaps because of her family's literary heritage and the admiration of her father-in-law Ch'ŏm, Nansŏrhŏn was enabled to pursue her talents in literature, painting, calligraphy, embroidery, and cooking for most, if not all her life.

As poet, Nansŏrhŏn saw herself in rivalry with classical Chinese poets, especially Li Bai, and she was a worthy competitor. She was able to achieve a level of formal craft in her poems her Chinese counterparts never did. With the exception of one character in line seven of the poem "Longing for a Fisherman's Simple Life," Hŏ kept all the rhythm rules required in all her hansi. Even among the most well-known Chinese poets, few achieved this level of craft.

Li Bai's poetry of mountains and rivers easily translates into the Korean experience of the world, given that there are probably more mountains than flatlands in the entire country. Like Li Bai, Korean traditional shamanism to this day reveres mountains as sacred places where powers of heaven meet with those of earth. This may be another reason Taoism and the Chinese literature that supported it was accepted by Nansŏrhŏn's family: it allowed identification with a cosmology that had been with the people of Korea for thousands of years.

In his translation of Li Bai's poems, David Hinton (here, following an older pronunciation of "Li Bai" as "Li Po") writes:

> The most essential quality of Li Po's work is the way in which *wu-wei* (doing nothing) spontaneity gives shape to his experience of the natural world. He is primarily engaged by the natural world in its wild, rather than domestic forms. Not only does the wild evoke wonder, it is also where the spontaneous energy of *tzu-jan* (self-so, being such of itself, natural, spontaneous) is clearly visible, energy with which Li Po identified. And the spontaneous movement of a Li Po poem literally enacts this identification, this belonging to earth in the fundamental sense of belonging to its processes. (xiii)

Nansŏrhŏn's poems inherited the kind of spontaneity present in Li Bai's poems, but her poems more often range themes of a domesticated world. Movement from detail to detail in Nansŏrhŏn's poetry builds to create an emotional energy the writer lives. It is not an energy she stands in awe of through a "self-other" dialectic, or an energy inspired by belonging to the world and its processes. The world around the speaker becomes—in the most felt moments of the poems—an instrument of her emotion. The writing is not only the voice of one who is alienated, but in contrast with Li Bai, is so alienated from the world the only processes she is able to engage in are her own. There is no belonging to the energy of the earth or its seasons and changes; the seasons and the vitality behind their changing is something one simply lives with, however joyfully or sorrowfully.

Other Influences and Themes

Nansŏrhŏn's writing is nuanced with han. Han, in Korean, is a private melancholy women experience from having a desire unfulfilled, or enduring hardship of some kind. Traditionally in Korea, women often express han by a long sigh or quiet tears. The difficulties of Nansŏrhŏn's life undoubtedly made her a writer utilizing themes and tones of han.

Asian scholars in the west have yet to fully consider Nansŏrhŏn as an inheritor of the "Women Poets of Anguish" in China. Following Kenneth Rexroth's use of Wade-Giles romanization, in Yu Hsuan-chi (mid 9th century) is resentment of sexual discrimination ("On a Visit to Ch'ung Chen Temple"), and there is Ch'ien T'ao's (early 11th century) "Written at a Party Where my Lord Gave Away a Thousand Bolts of Silk," which is comparable to stanzas II and III in Nansŏrhŏn's "A Poor Woman's Song." Chu Chung-hsien's (15th century) "Bamboo Branch Song" is a common enough title in classical Chinese poetry, but many of Nansŏrhŏn's poems resonate with every line of this poem by Chu. Of all the female poets in classical Chinese literature, Nansŏrhŏn shares the most with Li Ch'ing-chao (1084-1151).

Li was influenced by T'ang poetry, but the relationship between Li and Nansŏrhŏn is more than simply this. One could compare their lives: Li married into a family of scholar-poets, living what apparently was a happy marriage. During the Chin invasions of the 12th century, Li's family lost most of their material possessions, and her husband died soon after. Li then began to write poems about loneliness and turning to a mystical world of Taoist immortals, focusing on this theme more as she grew older. It is not known with certitude which poems Nansŏrhŏn wrote when, although there is little doubt Nansŏrhŏn wrote from her personal feelings, much like Li.

Nansŏrhŏn's sorrow (in her surviving poems) begins with her husband's absence, attempting to transform it into a song of faithfulness and endurance. This theme is familiar enough in both poetic traditions of Korea and China, but it seems likely Nansŏrhŏn, as did Li, slowly turned away from this motif, transforming it into her Taoist mystical poems as a compensation for the reality of her life.

Though significant portions of her life were removed from the world beyond her house walls, Nansŏrhŏn's poems are remarkably sympathetic to lower classes. It is easy to accept Nansŏrhŏn's perspective on life beyond her walls is strictly due to her literary readings, but this seems unlikely. Nansŏrhŏn writes about playing with friends beyond her house walls, and the kind of games they played were not typical of upper-class children raised in the capital city of Seoul. Judging from the kinds of games she played and where she played them, Nansŏrhŏn probably had friendships with children from social classes below her own. This speaks to the kind of culture Nansŏrhŏn was raised in and suggests a formative source for her willingness to accept difference in others, and a desire to be accepted for her differences.

Another contribution to Nansŏrhŏn's sympathies with the underprivileged were the times she lived in. The Chosŏn monarchs made frugality official policy; women were to avoid the use of gold except for special ceremonial purposes at court. Royal weddings, banquets and other court events often had their expenses reduced out of deference to the hardships of common people.

In what are apparently her later poems, Nansŏrhŏn focuses on turning away from the reality she was living and evokes the imagery and tone of a Taoist immortal realm. She chose these themes for several probable reasons. The themes naturally follow her T'ang Dynasty influences in poetry. Her blood family was knowledgeable of and had an abiding interest in Taoism. She read Taoism as a literary compensation for a life difficult to endure in the tradition of the Chinese Women Poets of Anguish—specifically the writings of Li Ch'ing-chao. Lastly, and perhaps most importantly, given all that Nansŏrhŏn had suffered and continued to suffer, she longed for a different world, one where she could have some element of freedom and happiness. She was able to invoke such a realm in her private inspired creative imagination, and it was a Taoist domain.

How Nansŏrhŏn's Poems Survived History

Considering Nansŏrhŏn's way of life and the events of her life, her brother, Kyosan, was probably Nansŏrhŏn's only continual colleague in poetry. The poems that survived Nansŏrhŏn had been long before given to Kyosan by Nansŏrhŏn as part of an ongoing writerly exchange of work.

After Nansŏrhŏn's death, Kyosan gave Wu Mingji, a writer from China, and later Lan Fangwei, a Chinese general, an anthology of Korean poets, which both men edited for their own versions of the collection. The anthologies contained poems by both men and women, including the poems of Nansŏrhŏn. Chinese scholars who read the anthologies were particularly responsive to Nansŏrhŏn's poems, so that when Zhu Zhifan, the Chinese ambassador to the Chosŏn court, came to Korea, he requested a collection of Nansŏrhŏn's poems. Zhu took a collection edited by Kyosan to China and distributed copies of selected poems to his acquaintances throughout China in 1606.

When Nansŏrhŏn died, some Chinese literati believed she became a Taoist immortal. Besides writing Chinese poems technically better than the greatest Chinese poets, when she was twenty-four Nansŏrhŏn correctly predicted the year of her death in the poem "In a Dream, Strolling Wide Mulberry Mountain: Prologue to a Poem." Chinese readers interpreted her talents and seeming precognitive ability as a sign of Nansŏrhŏn's supernatural powers.

Only after the Chinese popularized her did Korea begin to accept the possibility of Nansŏrhŏn's greatness as a poet. Kyosan asked several well-known scholar-poets to write an introduction to the collection he had edited: the Korean Prime Minister Ryu Sŏngryong, Zhu Zhifan, and Liang Younian, the Vice Ambassador of China to Korea. Kyosan published the collection in 1608 in Kongju, Ch'unchong Province, Korea, and Nansŏrhŏn began to earn her fame in the Korean literary tradition.

Feminism

Korean feminists look upon Nansŏrhŏn as a forerunner of women's advocacy in Korea because of the themes in her poetry. In the Chosŏn Dynasty, a woman who was not a kisaeng yet wrote accomplished, well-crafted poetry was dissenting against the society she lived in. The dissent may not have been confrontational, but the act of writing poetry, however private, was dissent. Nansŏrhŏn challenged Confucian misogynistic conventions not only in her writing but in her life. She occasionally left her compound unaccompanied for walks, for example; such behavior directly opposed the teachings of Korean Neo-Confucianism.

Because jealousy was grounds for divorce and exhibiting love or desire could lead to charges of unfaithfulness, Nansŏrhŏn had to couch the range of her poetic feelings in subtlety. Her poems describe the gender bias against women inherent in Korean society during her lifetime. She was able to do this without persecution because she held a small readership, and couched her language in forms that mimicked the poetry of traditional male poets. Anyone accusing Nansŏrhŏn of breaking social norms via the themes and topics of her writing could then be met with the defense of simply practicing forms and styles of traditional poetry.

Nansŏrhŏ's poem "The Four Seasons" rides the line of what could be published in Neo-Confucian Korea. It shows the facts of immediate circumstances only, despite an implied sequence of causes and effects leading to what must be the pains of jealousy: a woman desiring her lover-husband who has neglected her for other women ("Spring"). All three "In the Style of" (Shen, Cui, Li) poems have jealousy or neglect as a lesser theme, but because it could have been regarded as improper, Nansŏrhŏn borrowed the style of the poets to speak her feelings indirectly. The poem "In the Style of Shen Yazhi" demonstrates how Nansŏrhŏn expressed anti-Confucian feelings without persecution. The poem showcases Nansŏrhŏn's interpretation of Shen's craft methods, placing less emphasis on the speaker taking a walk alone, feelings of sexual desire, and loneliness—all of which were inappropriate according to the Confucian ethic of Nansŏrhŏn's time.

Other poems by Nansŏrhŏn were excluded from her collections for being too provocative ("Lotus Picking Poem" and "To My Husband Studying Books Near a River"). Some poems were, for the time, explicitly sexual (section XVII of "Palace Poem"). In the face of emotional repression, Nansŏrhŏn stands out as a poet who, breaking with the traditions of her time, wrote about subjects that were taboo for a sequestered noblewoman.

After her death, Nansŏrhŏn's poetry was read as a crime against the state. Her writings were cited as examples of the problematic ("anti-Confucian") thinking on the paternal side of her family, contributing to the exile and later execution of Nansŏrhŏn's younger brother, Kyosan. That a sequestered Korean noblewoman's poetry survived early 17th century Confucian political purges targeted at her family is a testament to its cultural value.

To date, no complete collection of Nansŏrhŏn's poetry exists in English translation. It is hoped this collection helps raise awareness on one of Korea's most important female poets, Nansŏrhŏn.

Translator's Note

Authored by a Korean noblewoman, the poetry and prose of *Spring Mountain* was originally written in hanmun. Hanmun is the Korean use of classical Chinese to write literature, and it was the primary language of written literature in 16th century Korea. Out of respect for the source text, *Spring Mountain* is a complete collection of Nansŏrhŏn's known poetry and prose translated from the original hanmun.

Hanmun poetry is structured around regular syntactical patterns that create semantic understanding. The same is true of hanmun prose. However, there are occasions when hanmun can be non-sequential in the flow of information; words and ideas can appear haphazard and, to a western reader, almost random.

Most of the poems and prose within *Spring Mountain* follow regular syntactical patterns of hanmun literature and generally flow naturally semantically. However, "Upon the Raising of the Frame for White Jade Pavilion in Great Galaxy Palace," written by Nansŏrhŏn at the age of eight, does have moments of semantic "haphazardness" in the source text. *Spring Mountain* is meant to provide a unified, sequential, and logical reading for the western general reader. As part of the translation process, portions of "Upon the Raising of the Frame for White Jade Pavilion in Great Galaxy Palace" have been edited to render the most welcoming reading experience for this book's intended audience.

—Ian Haight

Spring Mountain

Upon the Raising of the Frame for White Jade Pavilion in Great Galaxy Palace

I

Let me now tell of this.

On the moon, a cotton and ramie sunshade, hung high—
materializing vapors
from beyond the mind's
worldly boundaries
seem an auspicious sign.

II

If constructed on Earth, this silvery structure would shine in sunlight—
its columns the color of sundown's misty mauve;
and yet, this summery abode
will not be of the dusty illusions
within a bottled cosmos.

This royal edifice will manifest
as if the azure mussel opened its shell,
blew a mystical smoke,
and after the spout clears,
a palatial residence of exotic timber—
here on the moon.

Or, put another way,
this same residence will be built
by a divine being's conch shell,
which, when blown,
invokes a spirit, a highly-skilled builder.
Using this same magic,
the demigod owner of the conch shell

will tile the roof in luminant milky jade.

Or Blue Castle, an immortal of Heaven's fifth level,
will practice his magical art of lifting brocaded curtains,
and from behind them:
a complex of viewing platforms.

Or, similarly, the Prince of the East Sea
will open the cache of his lambent box
and remove a stately villa.

Therefore, from these examples,
this heavenly pavilion
will only be completed
by a power
outside the realm
of humans.

III

The owner's name—he who built this seasonal retreat—
is registered on a list of immortals—
position and rank,
among the superior Immortals of the Empyrean.

The owner
was an official of Heaven,
faithful and moral—
he governed the City of Opaline Twilight.
His status and reputation rank among the most sublime nobles,
and he was the most famous
among those in the office
of the Five-Colored Pearly-Haze.

As judge,
he punished Wu Kang

for violating Taoist doctrine,
Wu Kang, whom he forced to wield a steel ax
which radiated glacial-cold
from the hilt,
and cursed him
with an everlasting sleeplessness
to stand beneath a cinnamon tree
impervious to chopping.
Occasionally, the owner
enjoyed watching nymphs
dance to the melody
of "A Dress of Rainbows"—
some, silvery-white,
danced devotedly near the balustrades—
the nymphs,
with brilliant pendants of lilac star sapphires
that swayed
on their sleek lavender jackets,
and coronets
that glistered like starlight,
their hairpins spotted
with iridescent starry pearls.

When in Great Clarity Palace,
at dawn, this demigod would mount a dragon,
then leave for Penglai,
and at close of day,
slept at Fangzhang.
Sometimes this being flew upon a crane
between the Three Islands.
When the owner traveled, Fuqiu with his hengxiao
rode on the left,
and Hongya with his bamboo clapper
rode on the right.

For 1,000 years, the owner lived
a paradisical life

in ease,
but one day, fell
into the short illusion of humankind
on the dust of Earth,
because this immortal misunderstood Taoist doctrine
and practiced in error.
He was thus exiled
to Earth's Palace of Endless Pleasure.
Red Knot wove this connection,
and so, regrettably,
the owner of this spring-like place for viewing
entered the shack of mortality.

When friendless in the earthly realm,
in a room with taffeta curtains
and a silken screen,
sleeping companionless,
the owner may have fretted through the dead of night:
How can I ask a royal favor from the Palace of the Sun
so that I might make use of the Moon Palace?

He found a vial of an Elixir of Flight
and poured a little of the black sand
onto a waft of air.
Like a frightened silver-backed toad
that hops to its underground den,
the incandescent moon
declined into a lunar eclipse.
The owner smiled at this opportunity
to escape the sunlit scarlet grime
of his sublunary life,
and he passed through the ruddy murk
of nightfall,
through a passage to Heaven
from Earth,
an endless traverse, seemingly,
to Purple Palace—

to a banquet the owner had once attended—
a banquet with music
from deities:
marble chi flutes
and bamboo panpipes
evocatively played—
this party continued, in merriment,
as if the owner
had never left.

Yet again, I imagine the many divine beings
who attend
that ever-long event:

the Queen in her chariot,
drawn by cobalt-blue phoenixes,
a feathered parasol
preceding her retinue;
the herald of the King,
riding a milky-white tiger;
behind him
the procession members
follow a jeweled fasces;
Liu An, who wrote a book about divinities,
who summoned two dragons to his reading desk;
King Mu, who traveled west
to the Queen Mother
who lives there in the west,
in the land of demigods—
the king let his eight-horsed chariot
rest on a mountain slope
while he went to the palace revelry
in the upper worlds.

At daybreak, the Duchess Shang Yuan
is welcomed—
her combed blue-black hair

braided
into three chignons.

During the day,
the King of Heaven's daughter
is next received—
she who weaves
a nine-patterned gauze
on a bejeweled loom.

Such a multitude of divinities
gathered on a southern summit
at Diamond Lake:

the kings who assemble
under the Big Dipper
at the capital of the celestial cities
and Emperor Xuan
who, to get his feather robes of an immortal,
at Sen Zhang,
strolled with Gongyuan and his stave—
all attend.

The God of Water and the Immortal of Fire
who play Go
betting a planet on the game's outcome—
they attend.

The freeholder
received the Queen Mother
at the North Sea—
her wagonette,
drawn by speckled kirin,
arrived in the midst of balsamine.
Laozi, met at the gateway of China's western borders—
his powder-blue ox
on the lea.

The Immortal of Bees gives honey—
flies buzz
around pots of boiling jade—
an immortality brew.
The Immortal of Geese brings fruit—
in and out
of the glossy
blue-and-white
tiled kitchen,
he travels.

The nymphs Shuang Cheng,
with a mother-of-pearl inlaid flute,
and Yan Xiang
with a rosewood lute
produce a refined, noble melody
from mid-Heaven.
To this music of paradise,
Wan Hua
intones a piercing lyric,
and Fei Qiong
performs an elaborate dance.

A dragon's-head kettle
pours wine from the mouth,
the wine
fermented from the marrow
of a phoenix.
A tray shaped like a crane's back
holds seasoned dried goji berries.

One hundred invited spirits
will come from afar;
one thousand saints,
welcomed.

Still, this heavenly palace

of the upper worlds
is not large enough for everyone,
so a new one had to be built.

IV

There was no elegant seasonal retreat large enough,
so a new one had to be constructed—
how else would it be possible
for the Emperor of Heaven
to join such festivities?

Therefore, the proprietor
sent orders to ten lands
and across the nine seas
to collect builders.
A master craftsman
was given a nearby house,
and he selected the finest camphor and nanmu—
the mighty iron adzes and axes,
steadfast as mountains,
worked the pillar bases,
and the bronze levels and squares
shined an auric essence,
radiating throughout the heavens.
A granite forge, lightless-black,
melted iron in a crucible,
and the craftsmen
plumbed their measures
as skillfully
as Gongshu Ban.
A spirit of the earth
hammered his chisel
with utmost skill,
following ideas
like the father of carpentry,
Gongshu Ban.

V: A Reverie of Completion

A prismatic double rainbow
above the completed summery abode;
the ends seem to drink
from a coursing star stream;
the smaller iridescent bow
with redder bands
ascends
like the heads
of the six snapping turtles
that carry the Island of Immortals.

This elegant retreat,
singular,
bemisted:
an amber rafter
glows
in a sunbeam.
Beyond its paper-thin
white jade lattice and silk windows,
a meteor falls—
across from and level with the sky-blue corridor:
clouds upon the plain.

Nephrite roof tiles
sparkle
like scales of fish—
finely cut steps,
aligned
like geese in flight.
Cerise flags flutter
from bamboo poles—
other poles
with peacock feathers—
dense haze,
luminant

with moonlight.

Fu Bo, on the surrounding grounds,
raises a tent—
under the empyrean's three primary stars,
he hangs curtains
ornate
with fairy-slipper orchids;
others tie sun-yellow tassels
to the silkened windows of the retreat,
adding to the shimmering tassels
already tied—
a fine mesh net
protects the carved banisters
of the graceful summerhouse
from birds, insects, seeds,
and leaves of trees.

Immortals assemble inside—
within the structure
a painting of multi-colored phoenixes
emits chi.
A sylph stands by a window—
perfume overflows
from her mirrored cosmetics box
inlaid with the image
of two phoenixes.

A room of viewing windows
with pale blue drapes,
a peacock-blue jade wine table
behind a mica screen—
propitious waves of shimmering heat
ascend in the eventide.
This same room,
painted with lotus petals,
fanned by peacock feathers—

ivory-white reclining couches,
the room filled with delicacies—
a gracing spectrum of colors
over the building
all through the day.

In this edifice, the proprietor
will hold every revelry
with a revitalizing elegance
and humble, sincere
hospitality.

From the inlaid-with-lotus-engraved-jade balustrades,
dupion tapestry,
ornate with cumulous clouds—
from the gilt eaves,
amaranthine drapes hang.

Nine branches, each with a lantern:
the light falls calmly
upon a quilted brocade futon
and handwoven mat.
Virescent lotuses
and icy-white peaches
on plates, the plates,
embossed with images
of eight celestial oceans.

Only regret
the white-as-cranes marble lintel
lacks celebratory words.

The owner of the estate
asked some highly placed divine beings
to write their feelings
in a poem,
but, for example,

Li Bai, who dedicated poems
to the concubine of Emperor Xuan,
since long ago,
remains drunk
on the back
of a whale—
Li He, whose odes were written
on the Emperor of Heaven's
summery lookout tower,
now writes
with the absurdity
of the Snake God.

This new summerhouse
only bears
a small inscription
telling the story of its construction
engraved in iron,
written in the sophisticated calligraphy
of Shan Xuanqing.

The upper world pavilions
have beautiful engravings
from the illustrious Caishen,
whose style is
esteemed in history.

I feel shame
that I was, am, and will be
in the grime
of the lost human universe
in my lives
of the past, present, and future—
I have been falsely put on the demigod Jin Huang's list
for punishment,
and so am exiled
to Earth.

It is also true
that Jiang Lang's poetic talent
has been exhausted,
so the impression
of the five-colored blossom—
of his good writing—
ended.

This is why Jiang Lang pressed me for a poem.

The voices of past poets
echoed in my mind
in answer.

Slowly I held a vermillion brush
and smiled—
the paper, awash with ink
flowed with words
as a brook
is fed
by a spring.

It is not necessary
for the immortal Zi'an
to help these words—
the phrasing is so beautiful,
and passages, strong;
it is not necessary
to wash and sober Li Bai's face
so he can join
and help.

VI

Inspired, I present the divine verse
as if kept

in a brocade pouch—
this, the created ode
for this exquisite residence
with a splendid view.

Receiving the dedication,
craftsmen place all the verses
within a hollow
of the double beams,
and celebrants
now pay homage to the view
in each of the six directions:

The freeholder of the land
offers rice cakes to the east:
At sunrise,
may you, honored guest,
ride an ageless sage's sunbird
and enter Pearl Palace.
At first light,
sunbeams on the ground
under a mulberry
on the shorelines
of the Island of Immortals—
10,000 sun rays
redden
the bemisted day,
turn the ocean's surface
maroon.

Woodworkers offer cakes to the south:
May you rest
like a sacred dragon
with nothing to do—
one that drinks
from a pristine pond.
On a zitan bed,

drowse and wake
in the tulips' noon shade—
smiling,
call for a lovely servant girl
to aid in removing
your teal jacket.

Palace maids offer cakes to the west:
Covered by frost,
a petal from a celestial-blue ranunculus
wanes—
an iridescent firebird
cries.
Wearing a plain-woven silk jacket
for the season of rebirth,
embroidered with the character for jade,
a servant receives the Queen Mother—
later, astride a crane,
the Queen Mother
hurries
to arrive at her great celestial house,
though the sun's rays
have set.

The owner of the estate offers cakes to the north:
The North Star sinks
into the vast and wide North Sea—
the wings of an immortal bird
beat the upper firmament—
courses of wind increase.
A gloom of billows
portends rain
in the Nine Heavens.

Palace maids throw cakes upwards:
Daylight colors brighten a little—
feathery clouds hang like gossamer silk.

An eternal sage's reverie
floats around his hetian jade bed.
In the same way,
may you lie listening
to the Big Dipper,
the melodies
of the turning
suns.

Woodworkers throw cakes downwards:
Graying clouds
in the eight directions
portend
the night's
darkness—
a maid informs of the icy air
at Crystal Palace.
Frost has formed
on the rooftop tiles, the tiles
intricately carved
with mandarin ducks.

VII

As the pilings rose,
kneeling, I prayed:
May the cinnamon blossoms never age,
and the alluring fields of grass
enjoy a long springtime.
Though the sun and its luminescence
will someday weaken,
I wish you will enjoy touring
in a bronze-trimmed oaken chariot
and find evermore pleasure.

Though lands and seas change seasons,

drive that chariot
faster than a hurricane's current of air
and thrive
with a full life.

When the day's closing hazes
press against the latticed kesi-silk windows,
through a nearby gilded rosewood gate
inlaid with cobalt-blue jade,
look down over 90,000 li
and see the Earth,
small, hazy—

smile and look for 3,000 years
as the clean mulberry fields
yield
to the shores
of the sea.

Despite these burdens,
with your hand,
please turn the sphere of suns
in the Palace of Heavenly Paradise,
and may your body linger in the Nine Heavens,
despite the icy wafts of air.

Touch-Me-Not Finger Polish

Evening dew condenses on the bridal chamber's glazed vase—
ten fingers of a beauty, so thin, so long.
Grind flower petals with a bamboo pestle,
roll my painted nails in cabbage leaves,
tie them carefully by candlelight—
my earrings lightly chime.

Wake in the cosmetics room in dawn's darkness,
tie window curtains—
a pleasure to see Mars on my mirror's surface.

Picking flowers, a blush swallowtail flits away—
plucking my harp's strings, surprise
at the sudden falling
of the peach blossoms.
Powder my cheeks, braid and set my long hair—
hard tears near the river reeds.
Slowly, take a brush, and pencil my brows—
the brows fleck with nail polish
as from a soft red rain.

The Young Singer, Mochou

I

"Near Shicheng's stone walls I was born.
Raised inside the walls at the front of the town,
I played around the walls for pleasure.
I married a man from my walled town."

II

"I live in White Jade House—
my husband rides a quick horse.
At sunrise, in front of the stone town's gate,
we ply a two-sailed boat on the spring river."

In the Style of Cui Guofu

I

A wife wears a hairpin of gold
to show she is married.
Today, I give my pin to my husband
for remembering me over thousands of li.

II

On the lake's ragged watersides, willows grow thin—
an empress tree's leaves spiral to still water.
Beyond my window shutters, the quivering grind of cicada—
in this harvest-season air, a needling iciness above my frail, fine-spun sheets.

III

Vernal streams of rain drain the sun to mist over Hidden Pond—
a small shiver of wind stirs my lace drapes.
Listless near the little screen, dismal with the day—
beside the tree-canopied wall, apricot blossoms, splashed with droplets, fall.

The Four Seasons: Autumn

The season's chill creeps through my silk curtains. The long night endures;
the garden, stenciled with rime. My painted screen, cold.
Pond lotuses wither—their fragrance floats in night.
By the well, under the bare empress tree, no autumn shadows fall.
The sound of a water clock's *splish,* carried on west wind—
outside the door blind, on frost-covered land, evening insects sing.
On the loom, a sheet of cloth waits gold-scissor cutting.
In a cut dream, I saw you on the borderlands;
the silk curtains, still.
Sewing clothes to give to a distant officer—
lotus-petalled light, so frail, illuminates a darkened wall.
Holding my tears, writing yet one more letter—
the messenger departs in the morning through the south fields.

Clothes and letters finished, I walk my garden—
the sparkling radiance of stars, and dawn of Venus.
Under a frigid blanket, I turn again, sleepless—
slivers of lovely moonlight seep to a screen's panels.

Going to the Frontier

I

A beacon lights the Yellow River—
soldiers depart the capital.
They lean on spears, sleep in snow—
their horses charge to Mongol sands.

From the north, wind blows, jingles gilt trim clappers—
scolding winds from the border howl through castle horns.
Year after year, the horses chained, overlong—
all the pain, drawn out for war.

II

Last night, signal arrows flew—
a fortress, said to be surrounded.
Through a blizzard, borderland horns sounded—
the sharpest swords ran to Jin Wei Mountain.

Along the frontier, soldiers age quickly—
the horses, weak from long travels.
Men place value on chivalry—
return with heads from Helian.

Autumn Longing

Red curtains across the room
lit fiery
by the night lamp

I wake from a dream—
my silk sheets
half-empty.

This frosted night
the lovebirds converse
in their gilded cage—

the steps
thick with empress leaves
fallen in a west wind.

Deep Night Song

I

Cicadas sing mournfully—
the wind

desolate.
The essence of lotus blooms

decays
under an icy moon.

A beauty's hand
holds gold

scissors—
sewing a coat for war,

I raise the lamp's wick
through the long night.

II

The water clock
drips quietly.

My lamp burns bright.
Through silk curtains

cold nears
in the long autumn night.

Finish clothes for the border—
the scissors

cold.
Plantain shadows

fill the papered window.
The wind sharpens.

Lament of the Castle Builders

I

Men in thousands pound the ground with rammers—
from under earth resounds the *thoom thoom* sound.
Struggling with the necessity of good work,
on the borders, there is no generous governor.

II

We build a bulwark for the town, then build a rampart—
a high embankment slows the barbarians' attacks.
Fear only when they come in large numbers—
the walls will not stop them.

The Four Seasons: Winter

The water clock's copper bottles sequence the frozen night—
the silk curtains, lit by the moon;
my coverlet, cold.
Palace ravens scatter, surprised at a well bucket's splash.
Dawn's grayness penetrates the pavilion—
the paper windows, shadowed.
Before the blind, a maid in waiting pours from a golden urn—
in the jade basin, my hands freeze;
I smell the scent of lipstick.
Pencil-in eyebrows delicately, warm my hands with breaths—
the doves in the gilded cage hate the dawn frost!
Southern neighbors meet their friends,
they smile and talk—
a white face thins, missing a lover.
The wrought stove's charcoal warms a small silver flute—
below the curtains, his medicinal wine
invites spring.

Outside, leaning on a rail, yearning
for my lover on the borderlands—
he rides an iron horse with barbed spear
along the shorelines,
a blizzard of sand and snow blows, fraying his sable cloak—
surely, he remembers home—

my handkerchief,
so wet with tears.

Sensations of Spring

Far from his palatial villa, I grow disconsolate—
only letters come on the Han River.
Thrushes trill at daybreak through numbing rains—
a willow sways flirtatiously in the middle season of roses.

Weeds sprout from cracks, crumbling cleanly cut steps—
my elegant cither, blanketed by bone-white dust.
Who believes my guest will return in his pine boat?
At the river's docks, snowy-white water chestnuts in full flower.

Changgan Love

I

Changgan Village is my family's home—
I used to walk the Changgan Road.
Picking rose mallows there, I asked my husband
if my face were as lovely as the blossoms.

II

Last night, a south wind rose—
a boat with flags for Bashui came.
I met a man from the north who said
my husband was still on the river.

A Peddler's Song

I

I depart in the morning from Yizhou—
a headwind blows to the south.
On the boat's bow, whiskey wets our tongues—
under the rising moon, we row all together.

II

Wind gusts on the water—
three long days in swift cascades.
A young wife sits at the prow—
she burns incense to improve her trade.

III

Spread the sails, go along with the wind—
stop before the rapids!
Harsh waves on the western river—
how many days to Jingzhou?

To My Husband Studying Books near a River

Swallows skim roof tile edges
wheeling in pairs—
a rain of cherry petals
scatters in wind
pelts my dress.

From the women's quarters
my eyes search endlessly,
witness the sting of spring—

beside the brook,
to the summer-like fingers of grass
my adored
has not returned.

In the Style of Shen Yazhi

I

The pavilion glows rose in a late evening sun,
serene waves ripple the sapphire-blue pond.
Deep in a willow, an oriole sings, consummate—
dried sepals reel; swallows jitter.

A muddy lane dirties my gold-embroidered shoes—
a jade hairpin glitters from my bowed head.
Blood-warm sheets ripple in curves behind my screens—
I dream of love in spring colors.

II

A white pear blooms; spring rain falls—
night ends like a burnt red candle.
Above a well, ravens take flight at first light—
on a beam, swallows chirp in dawn wind.

Roll up my cool, windless curtains—
my chill quilted bed, so empty of anything.
Cloud-wagons drift, as if pulled by cranes—
east of the pavilion, a galaxy of stars, shimmering.

The Four Seasons: Spring

When apricots blossom, rain falls,
sinking deep in the garden—
a pair of orioles sing,
flitting in banks of magnolias.
A new wind in the silk curtains—
spring confronts the cold.
The lit incense burner
whirls a thread of scent.
A beauty ceases sleep,
freshening her face with makeup;
she wears perfumed silks,
fastening a jade belt
around embroidered ducks.
Draw the double curtains,
fold the fine green bedding,
take the silver harp, and casually play,
waiting for a lover.

Where have the golden bridle and carved saddle gone?
The caged doves whisper tenderly near my window.
Outside in my garden, a butterfly flutters,
disappearing in the bordering rose moss—
surprise lilies float in shimmering heat.
Beyond my flowerbed rails
the butterfly dances.

Whose house has flute songs from the pond pavilion,
moonlight on warm wine in a gold glass?
Through the empty night,
this anxious person cannot sleep.

At dawn
my handkerchief
wet with tears.

Xiaoxiang River Harp Song

Plantain leaves weep with the evening's dampness at a Xiaoxiang River bend—
nine peaks surmount the season's mellowing mists beneath Heaven's barrenness.
Under a river's lulling waves, perhaps the King, now a dragon, sings in his palace,
or perhaps, now on a cliff, his spirit casually plays a celestial song:
luminant vapors descend below the rim of his feather-plumed parasol, its pole, solid gold.
His wives of moon and flower hair mourn by the river—
not seeing him, their voices implore, like ringing jade.
A mountain parts two indigo birds from a phoenix—
clouds gather, blackening the river; moonlight weakens.
The somber sky's coruscant stars blur from streaks of clouds.

Walking by my gate, a fisherman sings a song of love—
the pond, silvered. I sit,
look upon the moon's half-light,
missing you.

In the Style of Li

I

My mirror darkens. Its phoenix no longer dances.
Crossbeams empty—the swallows have not returned.
My perfume's sweetness on a sheer scarf—
tears wet my silk pressed pleats.

A dream of adoration, of wandering a lakeside of orchids—
in Jing Province, low clouds over Powdered Palace.
The night's moon-mantle casts upon the river,
and perhaps a mountain near my lover.

II

My face, suffused with moon; I recline behind a phoenix-painted fan—
an airy spice of musk drifts from my dress of butterflies and peonies.
So entrancing, like Qin Province women—
even a general would weep for my countenance.

I gather spilt rouge in my silver cache,
change the evening incense in the gilded burner.
Watching river waters pass,
mizzling rain blends into banks of mist.

The Four Seasons: Summer

The zelkova's shadow blankets the ground—
an azalea's shade, thin.
In the high pavilion, a coverlet inlaid with jade
blankets my soft bed.
Sweat beads under my cool hemp clothes—
wind from my silk fan stirs the curtains.
From the top of deftly cut stairs,
I see the pomegranate trees, ripe with fruit;
sunlight shifts on shining eaves—
a blind's shade slants.
Swallows play with their fledglings
all day on a shaved crossbeam—
within the herb garden's fencing, only bees work.
Fatigue from embroidering—
the heaviness of sleep
rises at noon—
my phoenix-headed hairpin loosens on a silk cushion.

Sweat on my forehead cuts a fat scar from sleep—
an oriole calls up a love-dream.
On the south pond, my old friends in their wooden boats
row to shore, picking all the lotus flowers.
They sing a love song with their slow oar strokes—
two white seagulls, startled, take flight from the water.

To a Childhood Girlfriend

We built a thatched house near an old road,
we watched the wide river rush every day.
Now, my carved mirror has lost its luster—
in the flower garden, it is autumn for the butterflies.

On frosty sand, wild geese alight together—
in evening rain, a lone boat returns.
At night, I close a silk window—
how can we endure old memories of pleasure?

Love Poem

I

Headwaters of Kong Ling Rapids flow. Rain ends, clears:
haze expands over Wu Valley's endless turquoise.

My resentment of my lover's heart has no end.
It is not even like a tide, low in early morning,
swelling as evening comes.

II

In East Rang, in West Rang, cresting spring—
my husband's boat departed last year for Jiangling.

Black-headed langurs cry through the Bajian River Valley, woeful—
before three words can be spoken, my heart rends.

III

At home in Jiangling, my friends and I gathered
at the riverside stones. Not far from our house gates, water flows.
For play, I washed hemp clothes.

A fisherman moors his wooden boat
at first light of day.
I still envy the ducks, how they flew in pairs.

IV

Manifold rapids near the Palace of Endless Ease—
boats do not glide easily on the rapids.

Predictable tides come so naturally, regularly,
but once a lover's boat departs, when will it return?

The Resort of Fine Wines

I

Compassionate Yang Hu's memorial, washed with tears—
cattails cover the noon-day pond.
Was it Shan Jian, the later governor, who rode his horse drunk,
wore his white hat backwards?

II

In the morning, drunk from Xiangyang wine,
my gold whip cracks above the riverbank pubs.
Children clap and laugh, praising my horse's speed, singing its swiftness,
how like Shan Jian's silver-maned horse.

An Alluring Encounter

I

I meet a woman on a city street—
we share an erotic conversation.
Forget the King's errand!
I turn my horse, gallop forward.

II

Rendezvous under the tavern's sign—
hitch my horse to a weeping willow.
Laughing, I unbutton my otter coat,
trade it for the most sensual wine.

After Sunnei's Poem, "Wine and Women"

First sunlight settles upon burgundy railings.
I raise and hook the wooden shutters—

a thousand flowering lilacs
weave a cheerless seasonal tone.

My face already powdered,
but I remain, staring into a mirror.

Not wanting to leave the pavilion,
an unfinished dream lingers in my mind.

Who raises parrots in a confining cage?
I unbind the silk sashes, play a lute.

Lovely flesh-pink petals fall like feathers, wizen to dust—
all that can be done is endure.

I cannot bear grasping the silver basin
to wash my tear-stained cheeks.

A Jiangnan County Woman

I

South of the Yangtze, there's warm weather,
iridescent satin, and silver pendants inlaid with jade.
There, together, boys and girls gather water chestnuts—
together, they row their oars.

II

People say Jiangnan is a joyous land—
I live the grief in Jiangnan.
Year after year at a shallow port,
longing for a boat's return, my heart breaks.

III

At the full moon's first glisten on our lake's surface,
young men and women pick lotus seeds, return in the night's quiet.
Do not approach the shore—even with hushed oars—
mandarin ducks, surprised, might splash from the water.

IV

Raised in a riverside village
the young know no parting.
How could I know at fifteen
I would marry a common sailor?

V

Weave a skirt of ruddy lotus,
and a necklace of cream waterweed;
we moor our boats on a sandy bank,
await the frigid tide's ebb.

Resentment in Women's Quarters

I

Tie my silk skirt with a silk belt
covering tear trails.

Every year during blossoming spring
I resent Wang Son.

On the engraved lute
I finish playing "Longing for a Lover."

Rain strikes pear blossoms—
Close the door on the day.

II

Under the moon
autumn ends in the pavilion—
the painted paper screen

empty of feeling.
Ice coats fields of reeds—
evening geese alight.

Alone
I play the carved harp
where others cannot see—

a lotus corolla
falls
in the field pond.

Lotus Picking Poem

Streams of air ripple Long Lake
beneath blue autumn heavens—

in a place thick with tall flowering lotus
I tie my wooden skiff.

I meet a man throwing lotus seeds
across the water;

does anyone know
my half-a-day's shame?

An Enduring Mind's Song

Music flutters from a bamboo flute—
sun-reddened mist dissolves into dusk.
Raw black frost beyond my blinds—
inside, my parrot chitters.
Past midnight, a single candle illuminates my sash drapes—
occasionally, a meteor crosses a river of stars.
Splish from the town's silver water clock,
carried on west wind.
I hear the night tide insects converse—
Dew dampens the empress tree's arms.
Wearing a tight silk headband
for my mind's late-night distress—
tears from my reddening eyes
will surely stain
my pillow.

Remnants

I

An empress tree grew in Yiyang,
enduring years of frigid shade.
Fortunately, it met a master craftsman
who cut it for a black harp.

When the harp was played,
few understood the songs.
Finally, the old music
wisped away in smoke.

II

Two phoenix glide from their dwelling on Red Mountain—
the feathers of each, a rainbow mesh.
Portending virtue, soaring 1,000 lengths of a man,
they resound with the sun's song of morning.
The birds refuse millet rice,
preferring their food of bamboo fruit—

why do posturing owls and kites
nest in trees meant for phoenix?

III

I have one roll of silk.
I brush it gently, the sheen, still fabulous.

Face to face, two woven phoenix—
how brilliantly sewn, the patterns.

For years, stored in a case—
this morning, I give it to you, my husband.

I do not regret you tailoring trousers,
but never sew the silk for another woman's skirt.

IV

Pure gold, molded preciously,
crafts a resplendent crescent moon;

given by my husband's parents for marriage,
it binds my red silk skirt.

Today, my husband, I give you leave,
and endear you with a potpourri charm.

I won't mind you losing it in on the street,
but never tie it to another woman's breast.

V

My colleagues Ch'oe and Paek
learned by following high T'ang style;

Great Elegance was less favored,
but through them, the aesthetic has prospered.

Real poets do not crave power—
they are the lowest stack of firewood, serving on border steppes.

As they age, these men, having no influence, retire in droves—
I begin to believe true poets are all poor.

VI

Down the night, an immortal rides a saffron-feathered phoenix—
together, we fly to Penglai Island's Palace of the Dawn.

Scarlet banners ripple beneath drifting sea clouds—
a singing breeze snaps my dress.

Jade Lake's peak beckons—
the Queen of Goddesses offers a glass of immortals' wine.

With a borrowed bamboo stave,
I surmount Lotus Peak.

VII

A messenger came from the distance
delivering two carp.

I cut them deeply to see their insides
and found a piercing letter.

From the beginning, a longing—
the end asks, "How are the days?"

I read my husband's heart—
tears wet my dress sleeves.

VIII

Heavenly fragrant trees, luxurious in first lush leaves—
meadow sweet herbs decay predictably.

The plants of seeding spring, a natural flowering grace—
I am alone in this decrepit room.

A painting of five peaks upon the wall,
the Taoist book, *Distilling Compounds,* near my pillows—

boiling an elixir of life: if it works, success!
Again, I'll meet the King of Mountains.

A Young Man's Song

A young man should be faithful,
keep company with chivalrous men—
a jade brooch on his waist,
his midnight-blue coat, emblazoned with kirin.

In the morning, an audience with the King,
then a ride to the village, "Long Pleasure."
He buys and drinks the most succulent wine,
sitting among pretty flowers at sunset.

The gold whip overnights at a brothel—
his entertainment has no end.
No one pities the scholar, humbly sitting behind closed doors,
writing books on the origins of the cosmos.

Lakeside Song: I

Willows hang, threading the long banks for ten li—
over water, the scent of fully bloomed lotus envelops a traveler's clothes.
The moon's sublime luminescence mounts clouds, floats on the southern
        lake—
courtesans intone beloved poems, impassioned.

West Hill's Street of Pleasure

I

Wind-driven peonies bloom fully
in front of Mistress Suxiao's gate—

the scent of willows
in harmony with wine.

People toast to the time
with golden glasses, stroll drunkenly,

stay through late night—
her carriage of scarlet orchids

swiftly rendezvous under moonlight.

II

"Near Qiantang River is my house—
in May, the lotus bloom first.

My long black hair, loose—
I nod off, then wake—

in ease, I lean on railings,
sing 'Waves on the Shore.'"

Lakeside Song: II

I

Such large thorns—
lotus stems prick my clothes.

The sun sets along the shorelines—
the tide does not recede.

Lotus leaves crown my head
like flowers—

I tie lotus petals into a ring,
make a simple necklace.

II

The sweet smell
of red lotus
lingers

after weeklong windy rain—
women of beauty
sing

love songs
in rivalry.
Row back to the piers

of Heng Tang
at nightfall—
wooden oars

creak
from the depths
of mist.

The Courtesan Houses

Over 100,000 brothels
line narrow lanes.

Carriages
of seven incense-breathing woods
tarry
at each house's gate.

A whipping eastern wind
snaps
limbs of longing willows—

on a haughty horse's back
a man treads
on fallen flowers.

A Poor Woman's Song

I

Though just as lovely as others,
a good seamstress and weaver,
a young girl raised in a poor family
is never seen by the matchmakers.

II

She pretends not to be cold or hungry,
weaving below a window through the day.
Her parents alone have pity—
how could the neighbors ever know?

III

Weave without rest through the drawn-out night—
the wintry loom: *click-clack, click-clack.*
One roll of silk on the loom—
will it ever be anyone's clothes?

IV

Sharp scissors held in her hand,
the icy night numbs her ten fingers.
Sewing a wedding dress for another,
year after year, left to sleep alone.

Longing for a Fisherman's Simple House

Desolate eastern wind in my garden—
a pear tree, freshly flowered, near my stone and mortar wall.
I settle on level balustrades, remembering my home's waters—
I can never return.
Meadow grass on the horizon mingles into heavenly skies—
white curtains adorn my window aesthetically—
the iron latch, ashen-black.
Tears stream my scarlet-powdered cheeks,
mist forms among river pines—
will my longing ever end?
The wide river and high mountains—
these must be why
my husband has not come.

Small Lingering Joys: I

A snow orchid trembles near my window.
Once, its petals, fragrant—
brushed by an air of harvest,
the inflorescence wanes in frost.

The unfulfilled leaves, though lush, succumb.
The scent, so sweetly,
achingly, endures—
tears moisten my sleeves.

Night Vigil

With iron scissors, I trim silk
from the clothes chest.

Finished sewing winter clothes,
I breath-warm my hands.

At the edge of a lamp's shadow,
I undo my jade hairpin—

from liquid red candle wax,
I save a tiger moth.

Palace Poem

I

Below the Royal Barracks, first light of morning shines—
palace maids sweep dust from steps.
At noon in the Emperor's office, his words are read aloud—
behind a screen, someone calls for a scribe to quickly come.

II

The Emperor's sedan first visits a new palace complex—
a flute fanfare from the Office of Music announces his arrival.
Soldiers face the curved balustrades; their drums herald the Emperor at his
 duties—
through their song, palace maids announce the bloom of spring flowers.

III

I wrap green tea from the Valley of Health in a scarlet kerchief—
palace maids tie the ends in a blossom knot. I tilt the royal stamp
and moisten it with purple ink; on a scroll cover I write, "The Emperor's
 Word."
Eunuchs bring the tea to the ministers' houses.

IV

The wings of the newly-tamed parrots still ruffle—
I lock their golden cage. They nest in a pavilion carved with rose of Sharon.
Behind the papered door, the parrots turn their emerald-feathered heads to
 the Emperor
and speak with a country accent.

V

The exorcism ended, the court's maroon colors, aflame in torch light;
outside House of the Sun, the dawn bell sounds.
The Emperor receives New Year's blessings in House of the Dawn.
Sunlight shines on the crimson door: the nine ministers bow.

VI

At sunset, I lock the 1,000 gold embossed locks of the palace doors;
her cheeks powdered red, a maid serves the Emperor with utmost respect.
A eunuch brings the Emperor's summons to the maids' quarters—
questioning a maid again and again, he tries to know the Emperor's desires.

VII

In the wrought-iron stove, animal-bone charcoal heats my room, like
    spring—
my brows, shaped like mountains, still won't powder evenly.
So pleasant to wear room-warmed jade rings—
the palace of the Empress also has new charcoal, avoiding cold jewelry.

VIII

In autumn, nothing to do at the palace. Nights grow long.
The eunuch doesn't let me near the Emperor's bed.
Through the night, I hold scissors, cutting coruscant fabrics—
near a candle, I embroider violet mandarin ducks.

IX

At the Emperor's Mother's Palace, I wait at dawn for gates to open;
eunuchs bolt the Gate of Golden Locks and return to their offices.

I laugh to see other people coming—
who knows if we'll be able to enter this morning?

X

In the Pavilion of Incense, I find a maid applying makeup—
blessed with the Emperor's favor, she's separated by a new rank.
For the Emperor, privately, she plays a cotton-stringed harp—
that evening, a court lady brings her a dress of gossamer.

XI

With a court meeting adjourned, I avoid the sun at the Emperor's Mother's
        Palace—
first leaves from plantains almost touch the curved railings.
Leisurely, I play Go with the Emperor's Doctor—
I win a beaded jade hairpin.

XII

The Emperor's kitchen serves dinner on gold plates;
fragrant luscious fruits, the fish soup—it's difficult to rest my chopsticks!
I slowly call for extra food to be brought to Empress' Palace—
the maids on duty there are first to eat the honored food.

XIII

The bedding, too cold for a good dream—
I hold a silk fan, trace the flight of a firefly.
In Empress' Palace, the long-drawn night passes beneath a cloudless moon's
        emptiness—
wind from a western palace carries sounds of laughter.

XIV

Curtains of satin sewn with golden thread, a plush lilac sitting cushion—
but I am alone with subtle musk, my scent for enticing men.
Tomorrow, in a remote garden, I will enjoy flowers, and a sandalwood
sedan—
my servants now prepare the chair's mat and blinds.

XV

I look after the water pavilion and planting of lotus,
but at this moment, I carry silk from the Palace of Nine Gates.
I change into a gauze dress to meet the Emperor's messenger—
thick creases from sleeplessness in my blue-lined brows.

XVI

A palace maid pours water, douses ashes in her small, duck-shaped stove—
her makeup finished, she folds her cosmetics mirror closed.
Of late, the west garden is seldom strolled—
her jade flute and gold-leaf harp, half-covered in dust.

XVII

A newly-selected maid serves the Emperor's bed—
near a silk screen, the scents of sex.
Next morning, a eunuch asks about the night—
she smiles, points to a charm hanging near her breast.

XVIII

A gold gilt saddle, bridle of jade rings, and loose lavender reins—
the Emperor rides from West Palace to Palace of Eternity.

In the distance, he looks back to the south gate, opens a fan of pheasant
feathers—
sun shines on his overcoat, illumined red.

XIX

Busy with the Emperor's work in West Palace,
a maid of title passes through hallway doors.
Another maid holds a candle, reports to the Emperor's throne:
"The water clock has struck 1:00 a.m. at North Star Palace."

XX

At night, a eunuch brings a book from the library to a scholar;
the scholar takes a counter, folds back a page, and spreads the book.
With respect, the scholar tends the light of a golden lotus candlestick—
after walking to a sleeping room, he dismisses the attendant eunuch.

Tree Swing Poem

I

With my girlfriend neighbors,
I bet on who swings highest.

Tie my dress with an extra belt,
wear a headband: *prim as a mountain spirit!*

Wind lifts streamers towards the sky—
my jade pendant *clinks*

echoing
from a leafy stand of willows.

II

Finished kicking on the swing
wordlessly stepping down
I stand

take my cotton shoes
embroidered with gold moon orchids;
catch my breath.

A sheen of sweat
under my hemp jacket
sheer

as wings of cicada.
I forget to ask a friend
to bring my fallen hairpin.

On Shen Mengjun's Painting, "Windy Rain on the Sea"

A rainbow flares mid-sky, like a one-hundred chuk ladder—
barefoot mountain spirit walks the double rainbow.
Strong winds whip cliffs; the surge of swelling waves—
the sky, sombered by low clouds, bursts into rain.
In its mouth, a dragon holds a flaming marble
dives to an underwater palace—
a phoenix curls upwards on splendid wings,
disappears over the horizon.
A ghost wails, dissolving far into a cavernous palace—
the color brush overflows, deluged with passion.

Borrowing an Elder Brother's Poem for Seeing Star Temple

I

Clouds gather near peaks.
Lotus petals wet—
sunlit pines
on burnt umber cliffs
shimmer
with dewy light.
Noon prayers end
in an airy shrine. A service for the dead
ends in the main hall.
A monk begins meditation.
Cranes return to their pine tree nests.

Vines drape an old temple—
wraiths moan through the walls.
A sphinx lies sleeping
in an autumn pond. Dense fog
skims the surface.
Night advances.

Incense candles flicker upon a stone bench.
In the eastern forest, the moon dims.
A peal
from the temple bell
fades.

II

I wash the jade shrine clean
to celebrate
the King of Heaven.
In deep night

Venus
pale in a galaxy's river.
The floral scent of mountain nymphs
in their stocking feet
enjoying spring.
Water trickles
like tears of King Shun's widows
plucking harp strings
in night rain.
Wind in pines
carries a stiffening cold.
I dream an empty dream
in an empty room.

Zinnias, a scintillescent red in dew—
fog enshrouds a hilltop temple.
All day, my calm heart
fully awake
in samadhi—

I sit at a small table
in Sŏn meditation.

Small Lingering Joys: II

During daylight, no one's in the decrepit house,
though an owl, bold, hoots from a cluster of mulberry.
Iced moss covers a well-hewn footstep—
sparrows nest in the barren pavilion.

Wagons and horses often came to the stable—
today the house is a den for animals.
I understand now wise men's words—
I refuse to pursue honor or wealth.

For My Elder Brother to be Exiled on the Borderlands

To distant exile, an outcast
weakly walks to northern borderlands.
A young, but just Minister of the King's court—
though worthy of the King's love, why should he not receive it?

River water rolls calmly along shores of fallen leaves,
frontier mist burns with sunset.
The groan of freezing wind; geese retreat, like frightened children—
stop. This journey is not easy to complete.

Small Lingering Joys, III

In a Minister's house, the fire of power burns—
raucous music blows from his decorous pavilion.
Those of the northern district lack even rags to wear—
they starve in humble hovels.

One morning, the lavish pavilion lost influence—
the northerners became worthy of envy.
Prosperity declines in alternating times—
who can avoid this Heavenly principle?

Borrowing an Elder Brother's Poem
for Looking Back from a High Plateau's Pavilion

I

Below a mountain-peaked pavilion, a pillar presses
into earth.
In the northeast, drifts of clouds
lightly caress
the distant borders.

In Chulwon Valley, dragons long ago left
a newly-founded dynasty—
near nobles' tombs, burnt hues
of autumn. Geese pass
overhead.

A mountain range, lithsome,
limits the broad plateau, spreads across three counties—
a river cut
into nine canals
divides
the plain.

After my day's climb, I see
the sun's twilight—
overwhelmed, leaning on my sword's hilt,
I sing a forlorn song
friendless.

II

Atop a teetering ladder, I cut through clouds—
snow-tipped summits invade
the sky, mark Chinese lands. The range

ends near Three Rivers County—
the eastern landscape rolls
the rivers far away. A smudging
air of dust
wisps
into evening—
the lone castle of my friend
on the horizon.

Pastures of grass
please 10,000 horses,
fattened early for winter.
Looking east, a small keep beats its drums,
wishing to be led
by a cunning
general.

III

Ahead, the rock-ridden path rises into mountain mist—
my horse's hooves tread onward.
The trail ends.
I rest at the pinnacle, as if in the sky.
This late season of harvest
a dragon bellows from the depths
of water hollows.
Drizzling rain subsides.
An arc of colors glistens above falls.
A general's drums and flutes
beat
a hastened march
to the borders—
a prize princess, a token
of peace
for the Huns, intones
her sorrow

through lute strings.
Soldiers devoted to the King
sing "Leaving the Castle" at dusk—
their lotus-engraved swords
hungry
in petal-carved scabbards.

IV

Over 10,000 li, proudly,
the general's swords advance—
a white granite tower
crowns a mountain, stands
in slanting sunlight
in the sky.
A river streams west
along three counties—
a southern range bends, obscures
a plain's grasslands.
Clouds thicken, then rise below me—
in my eyes, the great ocean,
vague, distant—
climbing ever higher,
I turn back:
a horse from the borders
whinnies in wind
hungry for war.

Small Lingering Joys: IV

Last night in a dream, I climbed the Mountain of Eternity,
and barefoot, rode the Ge Pa Dragon.
An immortal carried an emerald staff—
he greeted me at Lotus Peak.

I looked then to the East Sea:
the surface, a polished consonance.
Below celestial blossoms, a phoenix warbled, flute-like—
a golden jar of wine nearby, infused with moon.

To an Exiled Brother

In a gloomed window, a silver candle wavers—
fireflies wane, flowing over the high pavilion.
The stunting ache of midnight
severs stems; autumn leaves scatter.

Letters rarely come from the borderlands.
Longing for the palace of the poet, there is no end
to the dead of night. The mountains, empty,
though the moon shines through my window vines.

Lament for Children

Last year, I lost my treasured daughter;
this year I've lost my beloved son.
Piercing tears throughout our family's land—
they lay side by side in their graves.

The emptiness of wind through white poplars—
candles of wispy lights glimmer among pines.
I scatter paper money
calling your souls with pure water
poured over your graves.

You will know each other's spirits—
every night, play together as you once did.
Though a child now grows in my womb
how long will it live?

Blank, I sing my tears,
bitterly breathing air.

Poem Given to a Nun While Staying in a Taoist Monastery

Mochou danced like a swallow, sang like a songbird—
at fifteen, she married the Duke of Bupyŭng:
he delighted in her harp of silver orchids.
She plucked the strings in his marbled house
wearing clover circlets—
she sang a serenade for courtship
in his pavilion carved with poetry.

Aglow, the moon suffused the resplendent villa—
in solitude, her flute-song entranced a sunbird.
Beyond her silkened windows, evening mist dissipated—
the carved lovebirds on her mirror wore smooth.

To have her husband's desire, on a secluded altar
she burns incense every dawn and dusk.

An ache of wind whispers
pregnant with the year's fruits
stirring feathers of a crane.

Regretting a Certain Emotion

A budding breeze lush with sun
unfolds a hundred hues of petals.
It is a season of prosperity—countless passions rise.
Deep in the women's quarters, I want my thoughts to stop.
Longing for a lover, my heart torn—
night advances, but still, I do not sleep;
I hear the cock's tireless crowing at dawn.
Silk curtains, unstirred at my room's floor—
moss grows on my windswept steps.
A candle's remaining light expires. I lean on a wall—
my silk blanket, loose, allows the bitter air.
I weave a poetic pattern on my sliding loom—
the incompleteness confounds my weary mind.
Life is governed by fate, and fate is both generous and greedy—
others enjoy life's pleasures, but I choose to be alone.

The Emperor Holds Religious Services at a Shrine to Heaven

The Emperor's feathered parasol progresses upward,
then stops at the viridian shrine;
on marbled steps at night,
tiny bells of his sedan ring.
How can one live a long life?
is the Emperor's question,
asked with veneration.

The answer to a long life,
divinely prescribed,
closely read.

Lilies and golden flower, moist in early mist—
the galaxy's river has long set.
Heavenly wind descends from the moon's mantle—
a crane calls in the winter-bound air.
Incense burned to ashes,
a bell resounds from beneath eaves—
thousands of fragrant trees
encircle curved balustrades of the shrine.

In a Dream, Strolling Wide Mulberry Mountain: Prologue to a Poem

Spring 1585, an acquaintance died, so I visited my uncle's house. At night, I dreamed of climbing an island mountain of multi-colored jade. Peak after peak of white and blue jade glistened, so dazzlingly bright I could not look at them. A dense cloud of rainbows floated above the mountains in brilliant colors.

Pure springs poured streams from the side of a cliff. The water fell between rocks, pittering like the sounds of necklace rings.

Two women of near the same age, about twenty, were surely the most beautiful of a generation. One wore a violet glowing dress, while the other wore a dress of emerald, the inside fabric, a multi-hued haze. In their hands, they held golden bottles shaped like the curves of a woman's body. They walked lightly on wooden sandals, and bowed to me.

They walked upwards along a winding stream, and I followed. Other-worldly flowers and grasses of a kind I could not name grew. Cranes, peacocks, phoenixes, and kingfishers all flew and pranced sprightly left and right. From the edge of a forest, ambrosial scents floated in the air around us.

At last, we reached the peak. From the south to the east was the sea, touching the sky's horizon, so that they became a single blue. The ocean washed the reddening sun as it rose.

A lucid lake lay in the mountain's peak. Sea-blue lotuses with wide leaves were half-withered by frost. The women said, "This is Wide Mulberry Mountain, the highest mountain in all ten directions of Heaven. You have affinity with mountain spirits, so you may dare to come here. Why not record this moment with a poem?"

I declined, but they would not accept my reluctance. I recited a poem in short form. The two women clapped and laughed, saying, "Every word is so heavenly!"

A crimson cloud drifted down from the middle of the sky and hung near the peak's summit. There was the sound of a drum—I woke, and tried to understand this dream. As if still dreaming, a smoky mist seemed to float near my pillow.

I wondered if Li Bai's poem "Strolling Heavenly Grandmother Mountain" reached the height of the poem in my dream. I decided to write down my dream's poem.

The Poem

A beryl-blue sea flows into a jade-green sea,
a peacock-colored phoenix mingles with a phoenix of golden opalescence.
Twenty-seven petals of a lotus succumb, bloom scarlet—
reflecting in ice, the moonlight, cold.

Sending Off a Palace Maid to a Taoist Temple

Goodbye to the palace. She leaves her courtly room of scholars.
No longer a scribe, her hairpiece changed for an immortal's luminous crown.

Time passes: she knows the boundless ocean, and naturally bestrides
    a phoenix—
there are no dreams in the Jade Fortress of Immortals.

Her phoenix easily takes flight—
gliding below clouds swollen with warmth

she shakes the hoary cold of snow from her lustrous gown.
Above clouds, the night's snowy light of moon—

her pendant charms resound in air.
Endlessly, she roams Heaven's sea of stars

wearing scarlet robes; happy,
like maids who serve the King.

Poem Written in a Dream

A mammoth turtle bears sacred mountains on the sea's horizon—
at dawn, six dragons swallow waves of nine rivers.
A pavilion floats near stars at Heaven's center—
the sun and moon never set in these lustrous upper worlds.

A golden kettle brims with a rose's sweet water of youth—
on a jade altar, a silvered crimson gown of immortals, luminescent.
Riding a swift crane to the Mountain of Eternity, my return, still too slow—
a flute's melody envelops a ripe peach for celestials.

Seeing Beyond This World

Chartreuse orchids wave
in a light breeze

a harpy harbinger wings above trees—
the Mother of Heaven
glides to an island
in a chariot drawn by kirin.

Later, in a phoenix-harnessed carriage of pearl,
wearing a lace waistcoat,
her banner of orchids coursing,
she smiles, leans over ruby trim,
plucks reeds of amethyst.
Nirvana's currents
blow sleeves of her citrine gown
into aureoles
the beryl rings
of her necklace *clink clink clink.*

On her moon-world
nymphs dance in pairs, strumming harps
and laurel blooms three times a year—
the winter-ending curls of clouds, sweet as honey nectar.

At daybreak, the party ends in a lotus pavilion—
from powdery swells of sea
an indigo messenger boy
rides a silvery crane.

A plum-colored piccolo trills
clears the hyacinth half-light—
the damp of early morning
sprinkles a universe of islands—
and the Dawn Star descends.

Walking Heaven

I

Borne by fleet phoenix wings, I descend
in the dark of night to the Island of Immortals,
then tour ambrosial blossoms
in a carriage drawn by unicorns.

The sea's slanting wind
shivers citrine-green peach petals—
on a little marble table,
an immortal's piled his jujubes.

II

My skirt, a scintillant nine rainbows,
my glossy jacket, weightless as gauze.
On a crane, in a fresh breeze of air,
I return to dream with mountain spirits.

Below a sunlit moon, the silk-smooth sea—
arms of a cosmos set.
My emerald flute riffles a melody
through drifting opalescent clouds.

The Life of Immortals

I

The Queen of Goddesses bids farewell to King Mu at the 1,000-year-old
Diamond Lake—
she sends her blue bird pages to herald her arrival at Emperor Liu's earthly
palace.
In upper worlds, flutes announce the dawn—
the Queen's maids await her return to Heaven, linger on white phoenixes.

II

Nine dragons reside in Red Jade Valley's Pearl Pond—
aquamarine clouds dampen and chill the green of Lotus Peak.
The Queen of the West's messenger and I fly upon birds with tail feathers
of rainbows—
we fly for her palace—but stop, stand before orchids of gold, bow to the
God of Rain.

III

The moon's cinnamon trees shimmer in the sublime sky's humidity—
from the sky's threshold, cinnamon blossoms fall to the trill of an amethyst
flute.
The Jade Emperor's messengers travel on golden tigers—
with flags of scarlet feathers, they journey to Pure Clarity Palace.

IV

Auspicious winds rustle lime-green, fine-as-sunset-mist skirts—
nymphs stand in their cloud-homes, grasp dizi flutes carved with phoenixes.
Beyond the distant hibiscus, a boy straddles a white tiger, whips him

forward—
at the Castle of Immortals, he meets Mao Zhong, his immortal younger brother.

V

At night, at an altar, Mo Ying burns incense—
a breeze stirs the plumes of his carriage; a breeze, cool on his sparkling, black-lined, white-as-cranes gown.
Porcelain chimes resound below cold-sparkled stars and moon—
beneath cinnamon petals wet with a fog of dew: a crimson phoenix.

VI

A party ends on a western terrace; the Big Dipper dims—
a red dragon soars south; a crane glides east.
In an immortal's room, a nymph slumbers from the heaviness of spring—
at daybreak, leaning on a vermillion rail, she does not return home.

VII

At the jeweled gate of my ice cellar, a few fallen plum blossoms—
mist moistens my silk hood.
The God of Spring no longer reconnoiters—
a scintillant kirin lounges near Diamond Lake.

VIII

A Queen's young handmaid opens an azure silken bag, removes *The Book of Strategies,* and reads—
humid wind hazes the moon: a cinnamon tree blooms into darkness.
Nothing to do in spring—
she politely requests a handmaid sing, "Walking Heaven."

IX

The brilliant, dream-like moon, gray-spotted with cinnamon trees; Earth,
blanketed by beneficent hazy-mist—
with a salmon and cream braided leather whip, an immortal drives a dragon
to court at the Emperor's Heavenly Palace.
Billows of cerise obscure the road; *who could find it now?*
At the immortal's home, after chasing ghosts, a short-tailed Shi Tzu stretches
on shaded grass, sleeps.

X

A crane rider in the overcast firmament has not returned to his dwelling—
celestial silhouettes settle upon his gem-encrusted gate.
Through the day, rain falls upon a stream—
Earth, veiled in blessed sweetness.

XI

In a lush garden, a maroon house, surrounded by boundless skies—
near a distillery for potions of immortality, a crane dozes in the night.
Ancient sages wake with sunrise, sing to the luminous silver-slippered
queen—
a little beyond the sea's pearly sunset, I hear a six-holed bamboo flute.

XII

Wintry air, wintry crescent of moon: the fathomless dark of night—
a radiant goddess smiles, takes her leave; she removes her flowered hairpin,
gives it to her lover.
He holds his gold whip again, points the way on the road—
on Jade Castle's westerly shores, a kaleidoscope of mottled sun.

XIII

A new order: the Goddess of the East marries Shu Lang—
through the world's vaporous mist, she rides a lilac phoenix to the Tree of
Sunrise.
Three-thousand years ago, before the blooming of peach trees, they parted—
she laments the immortals' world, where days and months pass slowly.

XIV

With my son and daughter, serenely, I bow in Jade Castle—
on the Mountain of Three Gods, everyone greets us.
Our dragon-drawn carriage stops; I stand beneath violet roses—
in the Violet Emperor's palace, I watch immortals play, how they throw
arrows into a pot.

XV

Starlit depths of a stream; moonlit beads of rain—
awkwardly, I tie my skirt ribbons, stand below emerald eaves.
On Red Hill, I depart, take leave of my feathered host—
he presents a string of hanging coral as a parting gift.

XVI

A sheeny gauze of heavenly mist moistens the firmament—
visiting Pure Child, I find her asleep.
On pale green paper, I stealthily copy a poem by the Emperor.
Pure Child wakes, opens her room's sapphire shutters—
the luminant moon and stars reflect on her terrace. Irises cast thin shade.

XVII

The Woman of the Western Galaxy lives alone, despondent—
the Emperor requests her to marry Secretary Hŏ.
She wears a glossy shan with a translucent jade belt, returns from the
Secretary's house late morning—
astride a sky-blue dragon, into the celadon-green sky, she smiles.

XVIII

Tranquil near Diamond Lake, I breathe the water's lilac sunset brume—
a gracing course of air stirs a peach tree's teal bough-blossoms.
I sometimes meet the eldest daughter of the King of the East—
all day before her portico, my bejeweled phoenix-drawn carriage awaits
my departure.

XIX

Shu Lang fills a sun-yellow crystal glass with wine from a gold decanter—
beneath indigo magnolias and the snowy moon, he offers a glass to a sylph
from the east.
Please, sister queens of Earth, do not envy their rendezvous—
they have so rarely met: only once in 10,000 years.

XX

Bored, restless, I dress in a sea-green qun,
climb terraced hills of Heaven; my sleek qun sweeps the ground, the ground
beclouded silvery-white.
Dewed camelias, like jewels on a tree, dampen my blouse hems—
by chance I find Pure Child in moonlight.

XXI

In clouds, an aquamarine dragon sounds a horn, pearled headband
on its brow—
the King of Heaven rides to Red Hill's endless light.
Taking my ease, I peer from a filigreed postern into the world of humans—
the land of China spread below: I observe a hovel's dot of autumn smoke.

XXII

I wear a crown of woven lotus, a waistcoat of ramie blooms, and a skirt,
prismatic in the sunset mist—
a mouth organ's melody trills, echoes around me in ultramarine effervescence.
An immortal's dragon's umbrage. The nicker of a human's horse. Near at
hand: the moon on the ocean's expanse—
I rise to Heaven's Islands of Immortals.

XXIII

A pavilion enshrouded by the murk of nightfall bears no sign of worldly
dust—
tears of loneliness wet the kerchief of Earth's loveliest concubine.
In cloudless skies, the moon descends into the gleam of a galaxy's star
stream—
parrots, discomforted by chill air, call for their keepers through
the darkness.

XXIV

My position in Heaven nearly secured, I ascend to Jade City—
the Jade Emperor bestows an immortal's title with a Talisman of
Nine Spirits.
Returning to my palace among cinnamon trees, I recline on a couch—
a white crane drowses peacefully near my incense burner.

XXV

Fog dissipates. The Emperor's wind-carriage lifts, arises into vaults
of Heaven.
The Queen arrives, tarries, then departs to the women's western kingdom.
The Emperor and his cerulean-flag bearing heralds return to his manor, find
its becalmed altar—
the moon, brilliant in dew-drizzled leafy peach blooms.

XXVI

The Emperor's Moon Palace: walls of milky jade—
before gilt folding screens, candles flicker in silver candlesticks. Evening
extends into lightlessness, uneventful.
Near the outside balustrades, cinnamon flowers glisten with droplets, cool—
an amethystine dizi sounds, emits an iridescent perfume.

XXVII

The God of Snow receives an earnest summons from Heaven's gateways—
riding a hoary ivory dragon, his glacial cold shivers bones of men.
Three-hundred measures of cream-colored powder in his sleeves—
as it scatters, snow flies, drifts to the world of humans.

XXVIII

The vast, everlasting Sea of Red Jade mirrors the aqua-blue arches
of Arcadia—
the Jade Goddess, silent: a sultry puff of eastern wind upon her back.
On the 3,000-li circle of Penglai Island, she wakes from a dream—
sleeves traced with weeping: the tiniest cut of her dream's sorrow
has wounded her heart.

XXIX

The River Goddess deftly sews a silvered carmine gown—
her ivory-white hand time and again snips with honed scissors.
Beneath the noon's cool cover of azaleas, her eyes scarred by sleeplessness—
the Emperor's messenger delivers a grace: grapes of peacock-blue.

XXX

Hua Biao arrived from Earth last night—
the scent of cinnamon trees wafts from his sheer ruqun.
Placidly, he alit from a crane to a courtyard of alabaster and gardenias—
sunrise ruddies a cedar forest; midnight's condensation, unabated.

XXXI

Forty years in a room hewn from granite in the Mountain of Radiant
    Flowers,
my elder brother tours the coruscant splendor of Heaven's empyrean.
We talk of human life, of straw raincoats in a drizzle of rain, and gudi flutes
    below the white orb of night—
I smile, point to the blond heather meadows of the Emperor's city south
    of the stream.

XXXII

Gou Ling strums his sapphire-studded sheng—
picking anemone chrysanthemums, he leans against Dong Shuangcheng.
He mistakenly plucks a lucent string of his lambent instrument—
in the distance, in the heat waves of dusk, the peal of laughter.

XXXIII

The Queen's phoenix-mounted heralds exit the ninth gate of the Palace of
Everlasting Clearness—
they bear her banners of sanguine and rainbowy feathers.
An appointment with the Crown Prince of King Ling of Zhou—
ice-blue peaches in bloom; he plays a bamboo reed at nightfall.

XXXIV

In the middle of a sea's expanse on an isle's beaches, the Tree of Sunrise:
a burgundy mulberry. How many times has it flowered?
My tufted aoqun of feathers ages into rags after my long excursion; I finally
have returned to my dwelling place.
Outside my eastern window, three long twigs of a budding willow—
I remember planting it after the God of the Universe bid me farewell.

XXXV

Driving our dragons and phoenixes forward to a meeting in a great house—
entering the effulgent celestial regions of Heaven, eight gateways open.
Before the King, the Historian of Heaven declares the King's proclamation:
the Prince of Nine Splendors Palace will preside over Kunlun Mountain.

XXXVI

The loneliness of the Goddess of Nymphs: at her stately home, a lone
phoenix engraved on her makeup mirror seemingly sympathizes—
in the spring twilight, in her chariot of clouds, she passes through portals
of Heaven.
Feng Zhi was a heartless man.
She enters her carriageway, cyan sleeves pocked by tears.

XXXVII

Pure Child lived as a widow for 1,000 years—
but now with Zhao Yu, she shares convivial friendship.
Melodies of nirvana through the eventide above the eaves, above the incandescent moon—
the Nymph of the Moon comes and offers congratulations.

XXXVIII

Passing divine pearly-white peonies, glossy on western cliffs,
Pei Hang's horse whickers on the road, and later again, upon a bridge.
Fortuitously, he finds the Jade Master's jade mortar—
an aura of cinnamon in a breath of phosphorescent moon: he adds to an immortality potion.

XXXIX

In the Eastern Palace, lower-ranked maids of Heaven come from their court assemblage—
below rose of Sharon, they gather, enter a valley.
Some casually recline; others play an immortal's iron yudi on a wind-cooled peak—
a puff of teal drifts, surrounds the Pavilion of Looking Out Unto Paradise.

XL

Upon a cloud, I arrive in Heaven—
lavender cattleyas burgeon near water on the shores of a field.
With a basket of red cherry, I pick dragon fruit—
I've forgotten my red silk whip to tame the cranes.

XLI

Immortals converge, walk a plain of heliotrope,
and eventually arrive at Pearl Pond; they pluck water lilies.
The flowers, moons in the gloaming. The Gatehouse of Arcadia closes—
the everlasting empyrean, misted in cobalt blue.

XLII

Lustrous sunflowers inumbrate my spruce Go board—
noon-day pines cast shadows upon our contemplative game.
On stream banks, the keeper of the Emperor's silver dragon places a new
wager—
at dusk, I mount the silver dragon, wing towards Lake of the Heavens.

XLIII

Overspread with refulgent vapor, the silvery brook of Pearl Valley—
the God of the Universe, fevered, rests at home, absent from court.
The Queen of the West reads him "Song of Clouds," then takes her leave—
in the afternoon sun, his bronze dragon dozes at his lattice gates.

XLIV

Astride a whale to Heaven, at the Jade Queen's castle, Li Bai bows to her—
the Queen of the East allows a party for him at Castle of Clouds to continue
overlong.
Grasping an ink brush, he composes a beautiful poem—
he writes well, as when, drunk, he dedicated poems to an Earthly Emperor's
concubine.

XLV

The Emperor builds a white jade pavilion—
the steps and pillars, pellucid, veiled in opaline mist.
Calmly, he summons Li He, who scribes the character for "Heaven" in a
time-honored style—
the calligraphy hangs high above the ruby-lined lintel.

XLVI

Lotus Castle, mantled in a silky scent of sandalwood—
by royal edict, Shi Manqing administers the maids' Lotus Houses.
Morning sun reveals 1,000 maidens in dragon-drawn carriages—
in a meadow of pearly-white orchids, the maids play an ensemble for the
taegŭm.

XLVII

The Emperor requests that Little Sunset Mist prepare
the Red Sand of Immortality on eight flowered bricks.
Finely sieved and caked coal heats mercury on a brass-gilded stove—
she fills a mother-of-pearl and jade tray with the Elixir of Immortality.

XLVIII

A nymph, selected as best among maids,
enjoys ten luscious peaches with the Queen of Goddesses.
Effortlessly, the nymph holds a brush, bristles of a frost rabbit's hairs,
whiter than her hand—
she boasts the bristles are from rabbits of the Moon World.

XLIX

A lord of Heaven rides west. When will he return?
His wife, the Lady of South Mountain, will soon come home.
Earnestly, she desires her tour through ten islands of sprites to end—
near midnight, announced to the tune of a qudi, on her crane, she arrives
home at the Mountain of Immortals.

L

Yesterday in Heaven, a letter from High Lute—
he writes, *The pink lotuses by Red Jade Pond have blossomed.*
Discreetly, I send a note with a messenger:
Tomorrow at sunset, we should meet at the patio in Sichuan Province.

LI

At the universe of Red Silk Palace, in her secluded sleeping quarters,
a lady longs for the King of Heaven.
Every peach petal of a tree has fallen by a stream—
the flowing waters, naturally, without intention, have freed Ruan Zhao
from time.

LII

We fly on dragons, then dine with dryads of Nine Peaks Mountain—
we depart for Eight Islands in the morning, and finish the inspection tour
at nighttime.
Late in the hours of darkness, we visit a class on a teacher's platform. Wind
and rains cease—
a young immortal flies home, whips his lightning-blue dragon to greater
speeds.

LIII

The Magistrate of Mandarins tranquilly rides a white-haired deer—
he picks narcissus, then climbs to the Pavilion of Five Clouds.
In the pavilion, the table's piled with books on Tao, the kettles brim with herbs—
how could this revered ageless immortal have frosty-white hair?

LIV

In the Emperor's palace, brick-red railings, emerald-green roof tiles, steps of Red Creek jasper—
the ground, overgrown with royal-blue moss, dyes our shoes indigo.
Here, I'm appointed Governess of Heaven's Eight Districts—
court meeting adjourned, immortals vie to bestow the best congratulations.

LV

From the sea's waves, raw currents of wind shake exquisite twigs—
the day closes in Heaven's capital as I look upon the king of flowers.
Urged onward through a golden bridle, a rose-red dragon pulls a wagon with satin blinds—
the wagon meant for me, now immortal.

LVI

A party on Heaven's Kunlun Mountain during the season of Heaven's fruiting peach trees:
glasses full of fine Claret wine; the Queen offers a glass to Duchess Shang Yuan.
On the Queen's behalf, I implore her messenger to travel swiftly east—
we desire the presence of old Xuan Yuan from Jade Peak.

LVII

Beneath my feet, the glister-dazzle of a starry host—
an island universe, lit by a moon, reflects on a wet dragon's lengthy mustache.
In a twilight drizzle, I smile, call to Dongfang Shuo,
Never steal the sweet peaches from the garden of ice.

LVIII

Springtime appears again around my ice cellar; cinnamon trees have
flowered—
alone, astride a phoenix, I leave a bank of vermeil in the evening.
Before a mountain, I meet Anqi—
within his sleeves, jujubes as big as melons.

LIX

The endless sweep of Red Jade Sea shimmers below the moon—
10,000 palace maids fly out upon pale teal phoenixes.
At first light, they draw up to a celebration beside Pearl Lake—
the tunes of tuliangs cool the clear blue sky.

LX

An ancient, wide-limbed empress tree: leaves luxuriant, dense with the energy
of dew—
the full moon casts a splendid gloom through the finely cut blinds of my
room.
I coax white rabbits to pound an elixir—
the mortar fills with the enticing fragrance of aloeswood and clover.

LXI

A message for the Emperor inscribed on pale blue rice paper, submitted
to a court meeting at Ten Walls Castle—
afterwards, from a crag's rill, we water our deer steeds while visiting
Shuquing.
Later still, after a banquet at North Star Palace, we return on cranes to our
residence—
in the upper firmament, our pendant-necklaces sound around the old moon.

LXII

Copper plates of osmanthus' dew, drenched in the light of three stars—
the luminescence of a setting constellation, low on my pale gray lacquered
screen.
My pet crane has flown off and not yet returned; I wait, refusing to sleep—
an arm of the solar system turns; starlight beads in my lily beds.

LXIII

The way to the Mountain of Immortals is across a thousand oceans—
500 years pass in one crossing.
Beneath cherry blossoms, I want to drink smooth Marselan wine—
do not let the blue bamboo change into a dragon; I wish no means to go to
Earth.

LXIV

Riding a cobalt-blue deer, I enter a valley of the Mountain of Immortals—
beneath wintersweet, every immortal smiles broadly.
In groups, they say how different among immortals I am:
It's as if Heaven's Seven Stars shine brightly on your forehead.

LXV

Bells below the eaves, silent; the gates of Pearl Palace close—
at Purple Pavilion, a chilling breeze as we sit upon reed and bamboo mats.
A lonely crane, startled by the full moon's disc on the boundless night sea—
the sound of a flute in turquoise clouds.

LXVI

The Goddess of Lands lives in Heaven's Jade Palace—
during the day, music from an immortal's party.
The Immortal of the North Sea, comparatively young, has an indolent mind—
he cannot finish drawing the Taoist Five Mountains on a thin silk screen.

LXVII

I follow Nong Yu, walking a street of Heaven—
beneath our legs, particles of dust do not spoil our shoes.
Ahead of us, thirty-eight kirin—
gold medallions adorn their horns.

LXVIII

At Purple Sun Palace in Heaven, maids bring the Elixir of Life—
the Queen Mother wishes a visit to Duke Mu's stately home.
On the way, below a window, I find Dongfang Shuo, who grins—
since we've left the orchard, the peach tree has blossomed six times.

LXIX

Alone at nightfall beside Diamond Lake, I miss the Emperor of Heaven—
the full moon illumines thirty-six peaks of the Sung Mountains.

I cease playing my phoenix-patterned xiao; the gray-blue skies of Heaven calm.
The Emperor in his palatial residence, so far from me. I cannot sleep.

LXX

The King of Heaven planted apricots 1,000 years ago—
on a twig, three blossoms in a brume of lapis-blue.
On occasion, a five-colored phoenix sojourns in the old garden—
there, I pick rhododendron flowers, bring them to the King.

LXXI

Before a shrine on Earth, clusters of enchanting aster with heads of crimson—
an immortal comes to see, parks his phoenix-drawn carriage.
Dust may spoil an orchid's raiment, yet the Island of Immortals remains distant—
with his jade whip, the immortal points to the far-away end of ocean clouds, shows his dragon steed where to go.

LXXII

In the morning, Feathered Man climbs a silver ladder, the ends of the rungs studded with turquoise—
in the sun, cinnamon trees among a cliff's rocks. An almond-white rooster crows.
Why does Following the Sun, a priest of Tao, enter his cottage just now?
Perhaps he was with Hou Yi's wife on the Moon World.

LXXIII

In the forest of sylphs, a current of moist air beguiles the flora and fauna with calm—
moonglow entices a naiad to a stone bridge.

In the amaranthine haze of evening, she leans upon the marble railings, will
not lift her head—
at Red Castle Mountain, near the southern shores, she longs for Wenxiao.

LXXIV

Master Sandy Field has closed the gates to his Red Castle Mountain—
surrounding Phoenix Pavilion: a blue-green forest, desolate, soundless.
The sandalwood scent of immortals dissipates at sunset as we walk
the cliff-lined valley floor before Heaven—
dew-drizzled cinnamon flowers, moonlit in the cold.

LXXV

Crimson flags, silky, unfurl in the dawn fog—
near a resplendent villa, after bathing, I wait for the Elders of the Five
Directions.
The autumnal waterfall looks and sounds like a string of ringing jade—
green peach blossoms engulf the Palace of the Purple Sun.

LXXVI

In spring, I relax with an immortal—
we do not notice the aging of the stars. Autumn alights.
Emperor Liu has not come, though jasmine blooms the ground—
the sky fills with a foggy dew; moonlight nears the pavilion.

LXXVII

A bridge of light to an airy residence, floating in firmament—
the Mountain of Nine Immortals reflects moonlight.
The Emperor's golden seal hangs from the horn of a kirin—
incandescence of moon chills the elegant, embossed letters.

LXXVIII

That sanguine candle, the moon, hangs radiant in the lower nine skies—
sunrise on manor steps, a marbled dragon statue, smoke from a stove's chimney.
At the Palace of Infinity, a company of phoenixes follows the Queen
Mother—
they come to salute the King of Heaven: *May he live until the end of time.*

LXXIX

At Terrapin Mountain, a low pall obscures the sunset's last rays—
like the raised blinds at Crystal Palace, autumn tides recede the ocean's waters.
Under moon-illumined flying cranes, aromas of maples: a year passes, as if
a dream—
The Spirit of Flowering Calyx, lovelorn, weeps at the Emperor's palace gates.

LXXX

The son of Heaven, God of Fortune and Fame, will go to a royal
residence—
his mother smiles, wants to see him, requests her retinue to prepare.
In a field of sacred lilies, her thirty-six shimmering phoenixes gather—
their aquamarine wings contrast with the lime-green lotuses of Willow Lake.

LXXXI

Hats woven from starlight, pendants of the gloaming's pearly haze add
dignity to their regality—
the Immortals of Three Islands have garnered me an audience with the King.
I strike my dragon's horn with my golden rod,
urging him forward, afraid of arriving late to Arcadia.

LXXXII

Eight horses of the mortal King Mu's enclosed chariot swiftly gallop to a celebration; he will not retire with the close of day—
a nymph of nirvana sings, waits, jealous of the Queen and her lover, King Mu.
In a Kunlun Mountain orchard, the nymph's red cedar lute resounds through the gloom—
her friends say she need not stay for him.

LXXXIII

Elm leaves fall; the galaxy's river flows—
midnight's beads of condensation cannot endure the harvest season.
Magpies scatter. There is no news of their divine bridge.
Vega looks emptily across the river at oxen drinking. Altair stands on the riverbanks.

LXXXIV

Golden leaves of trees whirl to pearly dew in the harvest season of Arcadia—
the Emperor hosts a ball at Five Clouds Pavilion.
Nymphs sing "A Dress of Rainbows";
winds of paradise rise, fill the world with the sweet sandalwood of immortals.

LXXXV

I ride a phoenix of rainbows, and at twilight, enter the Palace of Heaven—
the crescent moon, cinnamon tree-shaded, sparkles on Heaven's Jade Capital.
A starry host fills the empyrean; winds stir a paper-thin rainfall sheen—
an aqua-blue billow occasionally descends. I hear the song, "Walking Heaven."

LXXXVI

Removing her gold bracelet, E Lu Hua ties her satin skirt—
she takes ten sheets of a flower-print paper dyed by a cyan cloud.
A thousand years ago in the Palace of Singular Clarity, I made a promise on
 a terrace—
smiling, I remember the Queen's three bird-messengers sent for the immortal,
 Man of the Lamb.

LXXXVII

Walking the hazy-mist of dusk, I wear my glossy layered chima—
I call upon Ruan Zhao; together, we climb to a field of orchids.
A danso's song ends among the blooms—
in the world of humans, 10,000 years have passed.

Endnotes

IN A DREAM, STROLLING WIDE MULBERRY MOUNTAIN: PROLOGUE TO A POEM

The Poem: This poem is a prediction of Nansŏrhŏn's death at the age of twenty-seven. Some Chinese critics of the time took this apparently precognitive poem as evidence of Nansŏrhŏn's supernatural traits and that when she died, she really did become an immortal.

THE LIFE OF IMMORTALS

The voice speaking, days and places change in almost every section of this poem; each section is its own individual voice on the theme.

Section 7, line 1: Ice was a rare thing in 16th century Korea, except in winter. Ice also suggests the color white, as well as purity, the mystical, and the quality of being extraordinary.

Section 8, line 1: A bag recognizable to the 16th century reader as typically carrying books on mystical subjects. The book, titled *Yellow Stone's Book* (here translated as *The Book of Strategies*), was written upon silk and given by Yellow Stone, an immortal, to Zhang Lang (251-189 BCE), a strategist of the first emperor of the Han Dynasty. The book contained information on military strategy and longevity.

Section 12, line 2: A sign of favor. It also is an example of the sexual freedom in Heaven imagined by Nansŏrhŏn, as both males and females may have multiple relationships over eons of time.

Section 13, line 3: Peach blossoms were said to blossom every 3,000 years in Heaven.

Section 14, line 1: Refers to Nansŏrhŏn's deceased children.

Section 15, line 3: "Feathered host" is another name for an immortal.

Section 19, line 3: Here, the queens are earthly and mourning the loss of their husband who now lives in Heaven (see "Xiaoxiang River Song").

Section 43, line 3: A poem read during the meeting of King Mu in section 1 of this poem. The poem reads: "My home is where white clouds float in the sky/and the hillsides grow steep./Roads to here are long and distant,/beyond the mountains and streams./I hope you someday return to me."

Section 62, line 1: The water was believed to be an aid to immortality. The light of three stars was probably the belt of Orion, significant to East Asian shamanic traditions.

Section 64, line 4: Seven stars of the Big Dipper. The Stars of the Big Dipper have held an important place in shamanic cultures of Asia for tens of thousands of years.

Section 79, line 4: The spirit, an immortal named E Lu Hua (also referenced in section 86), waits for her lover, Yang, who will not come.

Section 83, line 3: According to legend, the magpies in Heaven make the bridge between Altair and Vega so the lovers can meet.

PALACE POEM

In classical Korean poetry, poems on palace life are rare. In old China, a palace maid was the only position wherein a woman could rise to be the equivalent of a Vice Minister. It has been said Nansŏrhŏn longed to be a palace maid (most likely a scribe) in China so she could more freely explore her talents. The series should be read as consecutive poems on the theme of palace maids in Han Dynasty China. The maid speaking, her rank, the days and places change in almost all the sections; each section is its own individual voice on the theme.

Section 1, line 4: This position of palace scribe was held by women. It was the highest position a woman could attain without being queen or concubine.

Section 3, line 4: In midsummer, the emperor gave a gift of ice to the ministers; here the season is probably spring.

Section 5, line 1: An exorcism was performed on the last day of the year to drive out evil spirits.

Line 2: The building traditionally was exposed to more sunlight than any other in the complex, hence its name, "House of the Sun." Most likely it was on a hill in the south part of the complex.

Line 3: House of the Dawn was a building for commemorating the first day of the new year.

Line 4: The door is the building's entranceway. It was painted bright red, a favorite color of the Chinese.

Section 6, line 3: The emperor's request for who would sleep with him.

Line 4: The eunuch asks how many times they have slept together and how much the emperor has enjoyed it. The maid's courtly rank depended on these matters.

Section 7, line 2: Although the room is warm, the season is still cold, so the woman's "winter skin" isn't receptive to makeup.

Line 4: Charcoal was available according to rank and favor.

Section 13, line 3: A palace for the empress when disfavored.

Line 4: A palace for concubines.

Section 14, line 2: The musk here is an extract from deer gland, most likely to win back the emperor's favor.

Section 20, line 2: This counter counts how many times the passage has been read for memorization.

Line 4: There is a scholar on duty until midnight in the palace. In this case, the eunuch has informed the scholar of a study break.

REMNANTS

Section 5, stanza 1, line 1: Ch'oe, (Ch'oe Kyŏngch'an (1539-83)), Paek (Paek Kwanghun (1537-82)) and I (pronounced "Yee" (I Tal (1561-1612))), all Korean, are called "The Three T'ang Style Poets" in the Korean literary tradition because they introduced T'ang poetry and the style to Korea. I was Nansŏrhŏn's teacher and a friend of her elder brother Hakok. In the 16th century, they were all part of a "new wave" of poetry in Korea.

Stanza 2, line 1: "Great Elegance" was an old poetry writing style in a collection of poems by Confucious.

Section 6, stanza 4, line 1: A walking stick carried by mountain spirits; "mountain spirits" is another name for Taoist immortals.

Section 7, stanza 1, line 2: Figuratively, a letter.

Stanza 2, line 1: Figuratively, "I read it eagerly and closely."

Stanza 3, line 2: Other possibilities include, "He said, 'I love you,' and asked how I was," or "and asked if I loved him too."

Section 8, stanza 3, line 1: The painting is a kind of talisman for bringing the "five lucks": long life, wealth, health, virtue, and peaceful death.

TOUCH-ME-NOT FINGER POLISH

Final three lines of poem: "Penciling my brows" is an epithet for a female poet.

UPON THE RAISING OF THE FRAME
FOR WHITE JADE PAVILION IN GREAT GALAXY PALACE

This poem was written by Nansŏrhŏn at the age of eight.

Section 5, stanza 4, line 3: The three stars refer to the belt of Orion.

Stanza 11, line 3: A new building required three inscriptions: one for the story of the construction, another which was a salutation to guests, and the third was the building's dedication.

Appendix I: Famous Names

Anqi: An immortal who lived 1,000 years after eating jujubes.

Caishen: Caishen lived from 1176-1230. He was a Neo-Confucianist whose teacher was the creator of Neo-Confucianism. Caishen wrote a commentary on the first scripture of China, *A Scripture of Documents,* by Confucius. Caishen wrote the commentary at the request of Confucius.

Dong Shuangcheng: A maiden of the Queen of Goddesses. She was reputed to ride a crane to Heaven while playing a flute after practicing Tao with Fei Qing, another maiden of the Queen of Goddesses.

Duchess Shang Yuan: Shang Yuan is the second highest goddess of Taoist Heaven.

Emperor Liu or Wu: Known by both names, he was an emperor of the Han Dynasty who wanted to be immortal.

Emperor Xuan: An Emperor of the T'ang Dynasty who, according to legend, visited the moon. After returning to Earth, Emperor Xuan asked his court to compose the kind of music he heard.

Feathered Man: The name of an immortal.

Fei Qiong: A nymph.

Feng Zhi: Feng Zhi was a strict scholar who, according to legend, lived in the T'ang Dynasty. A nymph visited him and proposed to him three times that they live in Heaven together, but each time Feng Zhi refused. After three years, he died and found her, the Goddess of Nymphs, in the other world. She sent him back to Earth, where he mourned her loss, regretting his decision.

Fuqiu: An immortal good at playing the mouth organ.

Gongshu: Gongshu Ban or Lu Ban was known as the father of Chinese carpenters. He invented many tools: saws, chisels, adzes, ink blocks, and weapons of war (castle assault ladders), among other devices and tools.

Gongyuan: An immortal who was Emperor Xuan's guide to the moon.

Gou Ling: King Ling of the Zhou Dynasty who ruled 571-545 BCE. A master of the mouth organ, he was reputed to play it as well as the calling of a phoenix.

High Lute: "Qin Gau" (High Lute), a famous lute player of Zhao, who became an immortal. He once entered a river to catch a young dragon, but surfaced on a red carp.

Hong Ya: An immortal good at playing the clapper, an instrument made of several wooden panels used to keep rhythm or conduct an orchestra.

Hua Biao: Hua Biao—literally "Notice Board"—was an immortal who visited his hometown on Earth after practicing Taoism. When he visited his hometown, he landed on the public notice board, and so earned that nickname from the local people he met. After seeing all the changes in his hometown, he returned to Heaven on a crane.

The Jade Emperor: The Emperor of Heaven.

The Jade Master: A man famous for making the Elixir of Immortality.

Jiang Lang: Jiang Lang or Jiang Yan (445-505) was a talented writer who had wide knowledge of many religions and philosophies. He also is remembered for having a complex writing style in poetry, and for losing his talent in his later years.

King Mu: A king (976-922 BCE) of the Zhou Dynasty who wanted to meet an immortal.

Li He: A prodigy poet, Li He (790-816) is often compared to Nansŏrhŏn.

He died at the age of twenty-seven, just as Nansŏrhŏn did. According to legend, Li was summoned to Heaven to write a poem for a new building erected by the Emperor of Heaven, "White Jade Pavilion." At the age of eight, Nansŏrhŏn wrote a poem with a similar title.

Liu An: Liu An (179-122 BCE) was a king and grandson of Liu Bang (256-195 BCE), the founder of the Han Dynasty. Liu An is remembered for inventing tofu. With the help of many scholars, he wrote a special book about immortals based on his inspired awareness.

Master Sandy Field: The name of an immortal.

Mo Ying: Mo Ying went to Hang Mountain at the age of eighteen and practiced Tao until he became an immortal.

Nong Yu: Nong Yu was the daughter of Duke Mu of the Qin Dynasty. She loved and married Xiao Shi, a good flute player, who taught her to play the instrument. During her playing, phoenixes were said to come and listen. According to legend, both Nong Yu and Xiao Shi eventually became immortals and went to Heaven, riding upon a dragon and phoenix.

Pei Hang: While sailing on a ship, Pei Hang met Lady Fan and gave her a poem. In return, she also gave him a poem, which in the last two lines said, "When you finish pounding the elixir and find Cloud Blossom,/you will become an immortal on the Indigo Bridge." On his journeys, Pei Hang met an old woman weaving, and asked for some water. Cloud Blossom brought the water, and Pei Hang fell in love with her. He asked for her hand in marriage, and the old woman said yes, on condition that he pound the Elixir of Immortality for one-hundred days in a jade mortar. After doing so, Pei Hang married Cloud Blossom, whose sister was Lady Fan. They all became immortals.

Pure Child: A nymph.

The Queen of the West: The Mother-Queen of all female immortals, the wife of the King of the East.

Red Knot: An immortal who made knots in the form of a man and woman,

their legs knotted together.
The River Goddess: The daughter of a king, according to legend, who invented fishing nets and cattle breeding.

Ruan Zhao: Liu Chen and Ruan Zhao of Shan County went to Tian Tai Mountain to gather herbs. There, they found a stream with a floating bowl of sesame rice. They decided to follow the stream up, and found two beautiful women. They stayed with the women for six months, but upon return to their homes, they found seven generations had passed. They had been living in the land of immortals.

Shi Manqing: A poet who became an immortal. He was said to like wine and was given charge of Lotus Castle.

Shuo Dongfang: A subject of Emperor Wu of the Han Dynasty, Shuo Dongfang was a writer and subject of many stories. Having great wit and wisdom, Dongfang stole three green peaches from Heaven's Queen of the West. Eating the peaches allowed him to live 3,000 years.

The Violet Emperor: Another name for the Emperor of Heaven.

Wan Hua: A nymph.

Wenxiao: Wenxiao (835 B.C.-?) was a scholar who loved Taoism, was handsome, and loved nature. Once he met a woman who secretly was a nymph, and she sang a song asking him to return to Heaven with her. He sang his answer of "yes," and followed her. The woman said they had karmic obstacles, and Heaven expelled them both to Earth. They lived humbly for ten years, then disappeared, riding tigers into the mountains.

Xuan Yuan: Another name for the legendary Yellow Emperor of China, said to have ruled China from 2697-2597 BCE.

Zhao Yu: According to Taoist legends, Zhao Yu was a calm man who loved reading and practicing Tao. In a repeating dream, he met a woman who wanted to be his wife. One day, a widowed nymph who wanted to marry him visited him, and eventually they did marry.

Bibliography

The Academy of Korean Studies. *A Chronological Table of Korean History*. Dongbang Media, 2004.
—. *Dictionary of Korean-Chinese Characters.* Tankook University Press, 2002.
—. *Encyclopedia of Korean Culture.* Dongbang Media, 2004.

Choe-Wall, Yang Hi. *Vision of a Phoenix*. Cornell University Press, 2003.
Choe, Wolhee and Constantine Contogenis, translators. *Songs of the Kisaeng.* BOA Editions, Ltd., 1997.
Ha, Kyŏngjin and T'aewŏn Ki. *Commentary on Korean Poems.* Asia Munhwasa, 1995.
Hinton, David, translator. *The Selected Poems of Li Po.* New Directions, 1996.
Hŏ, Kyŏngjin. *A Biography of Hŏ Kyun.* Dolbaesegae, 2002.
Hŏ, Kyŏngjin, editor. *The Collected Poems of Nansŏrhŏn.* Pyung Min Sa, 1999.
—. *The Selected Poems of Hŏ Pong.* Pyung Min Sa, 1996
.—. *The Selected Poems of Hŏ Kyun.* Pyung Min Sa, 1996.
—. *The Selected Poems of I Tal.* Pyung Min Sa, 1996.
Hŏ, Mija. *A Study on Hŏ, Nansŏrhŏn.* Sungsin University Press, 1984.
Kim, Changhwan, and Pang Yi. *Tai Ping Guangji.* Hakgobang, 2004.
Kim, Chiyŏng. *The World of Poems by Korean Poetesses.* Yeogang, 2002.
Kim, Myunghee. *The Literature of Hŏ Nansŏrhŏn.* Jibmoongdang, 1987.
—. New *Interpretations of Poems by Ms. Hŏ.* Yi Hoe, 2002.
Kim, Sŏn. *Hŏ Kyun, A Thunder.* Yaemoonlam, 2000.
Kim, Sŏngnam. *Hŏ, Nansŏrhŏn.* Dongmoonsun, 2003.
—. *A Study on the Poems of Hŏ, Nansŏrhŏn.* Somyung, 2002.
Kim-Shin, Myŏngsuk. *Hŏ, Nansŏrhŏn, A Novel.* Gumto, 1999.
Kubo, Noritada, and J. H. Yi. *Gods and Spirits of Taoism.* Puriwaipari, 2002.
Kwon, Kyŏgsam. *Commentary on Poems by Koreans.* Dah Woonsa, 2003.
Lee, Kibaek and Edward W. Wagner. *A New History of Korea.* Iljogak, 1984.
Li, Bai. *Yuefu Poems.* Translated by Okkyŏng Chin. Saram Gwa Chek, 1998.
Mun, Kyŏnghyŏn, translator. *The Collected Poems of Nansŏrhŏn.* Boryungak, 1972.
Nakai, Kenji. *The Words of Poems by Hŏ, Nansŏrhŏn.* Translated by Mija Hŏ. Kukhakjahryowon, 2003.
O, Haein, translator. *The Poems of Nansŏrhŏn.* Haein, 1980.

Owen, Stephen. *The Poetry of the Early T'ang.* Translated by Saehu Chang. Joong moon, 2000.

Pak, Samsu, translator. *Poems of Wang Wei.* Sekyesa, 1993.

Pak, Yŏngho. *The Literature and Taoism of Hŏ Kyun.* Taehaksa, 1999.

Pak, Yŏngkyu. *The Eunich and the Palace Maid.* Kimyoungsa, 2004.

Paludau, Ann. *A Chronicle of Chinese Emperors.* Translated by Tongchin Yi. Kangin Gongbang, 2004.

Rexroth, Kenneth, and Ling Chung, translators. *Women Poets of China.* New Directions, 1972.

Ryu, Wie. *Chinese Civilization in a New Light.* Translated by Yangsu Kim. Sigongsa, 2001.

Shan, Han. *Cold Mountain.* Translated by Burton Watson. Columbia University Press, 1970.

Shin, Myŏngho. *Palace Maid.* Sigongsa, 2004.

—. *The Culture of the Palace.* Dolbegae, 2002.

The Special Committee for Creating a Chinese-Korean Dictionary. *Chinese-Korean Dictionary.* Kyohaksa, 2004.

The Special Committee for Creating a Dictionary of Chinese Particles. *Dictionary of Chinese Particles.* Hyunmasa, 2003.

The Special Committee for Creating a Dictionary of Korean History. *Dictionary of Korean History.* Kyohaksa, 1985.

The Special Committee for Creating a Korean-English Dictionary of Cul ture and Language. *Korean-English Dictionary of Culture and Language.* Hansebin, 2003.

Tamagi, Ogawa. *An Introduction to Poems of the T'ang.* Translated by Kyŏngho Sim. Yihoe, 1998.

Yi, Ik. *A Book of Poems with Comments.* Translated by Sukki Choe. Wahwoo, 1996.

Yi, Songmi. *Fragrance, Elegance, and Virtue.* Daewonsa, 2002.

Yi, Yŏngju, translator. *Translations of the Early Poems of Du Fu.* Sol, 1999.

The Translators

Ian Haight's collection of poetry, *Celadon,* won Unicorn Press' First Book Prize. With T'aeyong Hŏ, he is the co-translator of *Spring Mountain: Complete Poems of Nansŏrhŏn* and *Homage to Green Tea* by the Korean monk, Ch'ŏi, both from White Pine Press. Other awards include Ninth Letter's Literary Award in Translation, and grants from the Daesan Foundation, the Korea Literary Translation Institute, and the Baroboin Buddhist Foundation. Poems, essays, interviews, reviews, microfiction and translations appear in *Barrow Street, Writer's Chronicle, Hyundai Buddhist News, Full Stop, MoonPark Review* and *The Poetry Review* (UK). For more information please visit ianhaight.com.

T'aeyong Hŏ has been awarded translation grants from the Daesan Foundation and Korea Literature Translation Institute. With Ian Haight, he is the co-translator of *Borderland Roads: Selected Poems of Kyun Hŏ*—finalist for KLTI's Grand Prix Prize—and *Magnolia and Lotus: Selected Poems of Hyesim* —finalist for ALTA's Stryk Prize. Working from the original classical Korean *hanmun,* T'aeyong's translations of Korean poetry have appeared in *Agni, New Orleans Review,* and *Prairie Schooner.*

Acknowledgments

"After Sunnei's Poem, 'Wine and Women'" and "A Jiangnan County Woman" were published in *Prarie Schooner.*

"An Alluring Encounter," "Borrowing an Elder Brother's Poem for Seeing Star Temple," "In a Dream, Strolling Wide Mulberry Mountain: Prologue to a Poem" and "The Poem" were published in *Asymptote.*

"Autumn Longing" was published in *Rhino.*

"Borrowing an Elder Brothers Poem for Looking Back from a High Plateau's Pavilion" was published in *Bombay Literary Magazine* and *The Meadow.*

"Changgan Love," "An Enduring Mind's Song," "Lotus Picking Poem," "Lakeside Song II" and "Seeing Beyond This World" were published in *Puerto del Sol.*

"The Courtesan Houses," "Touch-Me-Not Finger Polish," "Resentment in Women's Quarters" and "Sensations of Spring" were published in *New Orleans Review.*

"Deep Night Song," "A Poor Woman's Song," "Tree Swing Poem," "The Four Seasons," "In the Style of Shen Yazhi," "Longing for a Fisherman's Simple House" and "Seeing Beyond This World" were published in *Mezzo Cammin: Women Poets Timeline Project.*

"The Emperor Holds Religious Services at a Shrine to Heaven" and "Remnants: II" were published in *ZiN Daily.*

"For My Elder Brother to be Exiled on the Borderlands" and "Small Lingering Joys: II" were published in *underwater railroad.*

"The Four Seasons" was published in *Atlanta Review.*

"Going to the Frontier," "Lament of the Castle Builders," "Lament for Children," "Small Lingering Joys: II" and "The Young Singer, Mochu" were published in *BlazeVOX*.

"In the Style of Cui Guofu," "In the Style of Li," "Xiaoxiang River Harp Song," "Remnants, Part III," "To My Husband Studying Books near a River" and "Love Poem" were published in *Artful Dodge.*

"In the Style of Cui Guofu," "Lament for Children," "A Poor Woman's Song," "Remnants" and "Small Lingering Joys" were published in *Pitkin in Progress.*

"Lakeside Song: I," "Remnants: IV" and "Small Lingering Joys: I" were published in *Sublunary.*

"Lament for Children" was published in *Arkana.*

"The Life of Immortals" was published in *Infinity Wanderers.*

"The Life of Immortals: XVI, XVIII, XXI, XXII, XXVI, XXVII, XLI" were published in *Paris LitUp.*

"Night Vigil" was published in *Asheville Poetry Review.*

"On Shen Mengjun's Painting, 'Windy Rain on the Sea,'" "A Peddler's Song," "West Hill's Street of Pleasure" and "Sending off a Palace Maid to a Taoist Temple" were published in *Loch Raven Review.*

"Palace Poem: I-IX" was published in *Agni.*

"Palace Poem: XI-XX" was published in *Copihue* and *Quarterly West.*

"Poem Given to a Nun While Staying in a Taoist Monastery" was published in *Ninth Letter* (Winner of the Literature in Translation Prize).

"Poem Written in a Dream," "Small Lingering Joys: IV," "Walking Heaven," "Remnants: VI" and "Remnants: VIII" were published in *Azona*L

"Regretting a Certain Emotion" and "To a Childhood Girlfriend" were published in *Structo.*

"Remnants, Part I," "Remnants, Part V," "A Young Man's Song" and "Small Lingering Joys, Part III" were published in *The Poetry Review* (UK).
"Remnants, Part VII" and "The Resort of Fine Wines" were published in *Blue Unicorn.*

"To an Exiled Brother" was published in *Runes, Pitkin in Progress* and *JoongAng Daily News.*

"Upon the Raising of the Frame for White Jade Pavilion" was published in *State of Matter.*

Thank you Beatrix Gates and Ann E. Michael for writing wisdom.